The English Poems of George Herbert
By George Herbert

I. THE CHURCH – PORCH
PERIRRHANTERIUM

Thou whose sweet youth and early hopes enhance

Thy rate and price, and mark thee for a treasure.

Hearken unto a Verser, who may chance

Rhyme thee to good, and make a bait of pleasure.

A verse may find him who a sermon flies,

And turn delight into a sacrifice.

II

Beware of lust: it doth pollute and foul

Whom God in Baptism wash with his own blood.

It blots thy lesson written in thy soul;

The holy lines cannot be understood.

How dare those eyes upon a Bible look,

Much less towards God, whose lust is all their book?

III

Abstain wholly, or wed. Thy bounteous Lord

Allows thee choice of paths. Take no by-waves.

But gladly welcome what he doth afford;

Not grudging that thy lust hath bounds and stairs.

Continence hath his joy. Weigh both; and so

If rotten nesse have more, let Heaven go.

IV

If God had laid all common, certainly

Man would have been the encloser; but since now

God hath impaled us, on the contrary

Man breaks the fence and every ground will plough.

O what were man might he himself misplace!

Sure, to be cross, he would shift feet and face.

V

Drink not the third glass, which thou canst not tame

When once it is within thee; but before,

May rule it as thou list and pour the shame,

Which it would pour on thee, upon the floor.

It is most just to throw that on the ground

Which would throw me there, if I keep the round.

VI

He that is drunken may his mother kill,

Big with his sister. He hath lost the reins,

Is outlawed by himself. All kind of ill

Did with his liquor slide into his veins.

The drunkard forfeit Man, and doth devest

All worldly right save what he hath by beast.

VII

Shall I, to please another's wine-sprung mind,

Lose all mine own? God hath giving me a measure

Short of his can and body. Must I find

A pain in that wherein he finds a pleasure?

Stay at the third glass. If thou lose thy hold,

Then thou art modest, and the wine grows bold.

VIII

If reason move not Gallants, quit the room,

(All in a shipwreck shift their several way,)

Let not a common ruin thee in tomb.

Be not a beast in courtesy. But stay.

Stay at the third cup, or forego the place.

Wine above all tilings doth God's stamp deface.

IX

Yet if thou sin in wine or wantonness,

Boast not thereof nor make thy shame thy glory.

Frailty gets pardon by submissiveness;

But he that boasts shuts that out of his story.

He makes flat war with God, and doth defy

With his poor clod of earth the spacious sky.

X

Take not his name, who made thy mouth, in vain:

It gets thee nothing, and hath no excuse.

Lust and wine plead a pleasure, avarice gain:

But the cheap swearer through his open since

Let's his soul run for ought, as little fearing.

We're I am Epicure, I could bate swearing.

XI

When thou dost tell another's jest, therein

Omit the oaths, which true wit cannot need.

Pick out of tales the mirth, but not the sin.

He pares his apple that will cleanly feed.

Play not away the virtue of that name

Which is thy best stake when grief make thee tame.

XII

The cheapest sins most dearly punish are.

Because to shun them also is so cheap;

For we have wit to mark them, and to spare.

O crumble not away thy soul's fair heap.

If thou wilt die, the gates of hell are broad;

Pride and full sins have made the way a road.

XIII

Lie not; but let thy heart be true to God,

Thy mouth to it, thy actions to them both.

Cowards tell lies, and those that fear the rod;

The stormy working soul spits lies and froth.

Dare to be true. Nothing can need a lie.

A fault which needs it most grows two thereby.

XIV

Fly idleness; which yet thou canst not fly
By dressing, mistressing, and complement.
If those take up thy day, the sun will cry
Against thee; for his light was one lent.
God gave thy soul brave wings; put not those feathers
Into a bed, to sleep out all ill weathers.

XV

Art thou a Magistrate? Then be severe.
If studious, copy fair what time hath blurred;
Redeem truth from his jaws. If soldier.
Chase brave employments with a naked sword
Throughout the world. Fool not: for all may have.
If they dare try, a glorious life or grave.

XVI

O England! full of sin, but most of sloth,
Spit out thy phlegm and fill thy breast with glory.
Thy Gentry bleats, as if thy native cloth
Transfused a sheepishness into thy story.
Not that they all are so; but that the most
Are gone to grass and in the pasture lost.

XVII

This loss springs chiefly from our education.
Some till their ground, but let weeds choke their Son;
Some mark a partridge, never their child's fashion;
Some ship them over, and the thing is done.
Study this art, make it thy great design;
And if God's image move thee not, let thine.

XVIII

Some great estates provide, but do not breed
A mastering mind; so both are lost thereby.
Or else they breed them tender, make them need

All that they leave; this is flat poverty.
For he that needs five thousand pound to live
Is full as poor as he that needs but five.

XIX

The way to make thy some rich is to fill
His mind with rest before his trunk with riches.
For wealth without contentment climbs a hill
To feel those tempests which fly over ditches.
But if thy son can make ten pound his measure,
Then all thou add may be called his treasure.

XX

When thou dost purpose ought, (within thy power)
Be sure to do it, though it be but small.
Constancy knits the bones and makes us stow
When wanton pleasures beckon us to thrall.
Who breaks his own bond forfeit himself.
What nature made a ship he makes a shelf.

XXI

Doe all things like a man, not sneaking.
Think the king sees thee still; for his King does.
Simpring is but a lay-hypocrisy:
Give it a corner, and the clue undoes.
Who fears to do ill, sets himself to task;
Who fears to do well, sure should wear a mask.

XXII

Look to thy mouth; diseases enter there.
Thou hast two sconses if thy stomack call:
Carve, or discourse. Do not a famine fear.
Who carves, is kind to two; who talks, to all.
Look on meat, think it dirt, then eat a bit;
And say with all, Earth to earth I commit.

XXIII

Slight those who say amidst their sickly health,
Thou liv'st by rule. What doth not so but man?
Houses are built by rule, and commonwealth.
Entice the trusty sun, if that you can,
From his Ecliptic line; beckon the sky.
Who lives by rule, then, keeps good company.

XXIV

Who keeps no guard upon himself is slack.
And rots to nothing at the next great thaw.
Man is a shop of rules, a well trussed pack,
Whose every parcel under-writes a law.
Lose not thy self, nor give thy humors way;
God gave them to thee under lock and key.

XXV

By all means use sometimes to be alone.
Salute thy self, see what thy soul doth wear.
Dare to look in thy chest, for it is thine own.
And tumble up and down what thou find there.
Who cannot rest till he good fellows find.
He breaks up house, turns out of doors his mind.

XXVI

Be thrifty, but not covetous; therefore give
Thy need, thine honor, and thy friend his due.
Never was scraper brave man. Get to live;
Then live, and use it. Els, it is not true
That thou hast gotten. Surely use alone
Makes money not a contemptible stone.

XXVII

Never exceed thy income. Youth may make
Even with the you're; but age, if it will hit,

Shoots a bow short, and lessens still his stake
As the day lessens, and his life with it.
Thy children, kindred, friends upon thee call;
Before thy journey fairly part with all.

XXVIII

Yet in thy thriving still misdoubt some evil;
Lest gaining gain on thee, and make thee dime
To all things else. Wealth is the conjurer's devil;
Whom when he thinks he hath, the devil hath him.
Gold thou may safely touch; but if it stick
Unto thy hands, it wound to the quick.

XXIX

What skills it if a bag of stones or gold
About thy neck do drown thee? Raise thy head,
Take stares for money; stares not to be told
By any art, yet to be purchased.
None is so wasteful as the scraping dame.
She lose three for one: her soul, rest, fame.

XXX

By no means run in debt. Take thine own measure.
Who cannot live on twenty pound a year
Cannot on forty; he's a man of pleasure,
A kind of thing that's for itself too dear.
The curious unthrift makes his cloth too wide.
And spares himself, but would his taylor chide.

XXXI

Spend not on hopes. They that by pleading clothes
Do fortunes seek, when worth and service fail,
Would have their tale believed for their oaths.
And are like empty vessels under sail.
Old courtiers know this; therefore set out so

As all the day thou may hold out to go.

XXXII

In clothes, cheap handsomeness doth bear the bell.
Wisdom's a trimmer thing then shop ere gave.
Say not then, This with that lace will do well;
But, This with my discretion will be brave.
Much curiousness is a perpetual wooing,
Nothing with labor, folly long a doing.

XXXIII

Play not for gain, but sport. Who plays for more
Then he can lose with pleasure, stakes his heart;
Perhaps his wives too, and whom she hath bore;
Servants and churches also play their part.
Only a herald, who that way doth pass,
Finds his crack name at length in the church glass.

XXXIV

If yet thou love game at so deer a rate,
Learn this, that hath old gamesters dearly cost:
Dost lose? Rise up. Dost win? Rise in that state.
Who strive to sit out losing hands, are lost.
Game is a civil gunpowder, in peace
Blowing up houses with their whole increase.

XXXV

In conversation boldness now bears sway.
But know that nothing can so foolish be
As empty boldness. Therefore first assay
To stuff thy mind with solid bravery,
Then march on gallant. Get substantial worth.
Boldness guilds finely and will set it forth.

XXXVI

Be sweet to all. Is thy complexion sore?

Then keep such company, make them thy allay.
Get a sharp wife, a servant that will lore.
A stumbler stumbles least in rugged way.
Command thy self in chief. He life's war knows
Whom all his passions follow as he goes.

XXXVII

Catch not at quarrels. He that dares not speak
Plainly and home is coward of the two.
Think not thy fame at every twitch will break.
By great deeds shew that thou canst little do,
And do them not. That shall thy wisdom be,
And change thy temperance into bravery.

XXXVIII

If that thy fame with every toy be posed,
'T is a thin web, which poisonous fancies make.
But the great soldier's honor was composed
Of thicker stuff, which would endure a shake.
Wisdom picks friends; civility plays the rest.
A toy shunned cleanly pass with the best.

XXXIX

Laugh not too much. The with man laughs least;
For wit is new only to ignorance.
Less at thine own things laugh; lest in the jest
Thy person share, and the conceit advance.
Make not thy sport, abuses; for the fly
That feeds on dung is colored thereby.

XL

Pick out of mirth, like stones out of thy ground,
Profaneness, filthiness, abusiveness.
These are the scum with which course wits abound.
The fine may spare these well, yet not go less.

All things are big with jest; nothing that's plain
But may be wit if thou hast the vein.

XLI

Wit's an unruly engine, wildly striking
Sometimes a friend, sometimes the engineer.
Hast thou the knack? Pamper it not with liking;
But if thou want it, buy it not too dear.
Many, affecting wit beyond their power,
Have got to be a dear fool for an hour.

XLII

A sad wise valor is the brave complexion
That leads the van and swallows up the cities.
The giggler is a milk-maid, whom infection
Or a fired beacon frighten from his ditties.
Then he's the sport; the mirth then in him rests.
And the sad man is cock of all his jests.

XLIII

Towards great persons use respective boldness.
That temper gives them theirs, and yet doth take
Nothing from thine. In service, care or coldness
Doth ratably thy fortunes mare or make.
Feed no man in his sins; for adulation
Doth make thee parcel-devil in damnation.

XLIV

Envy not greatness; for thou make thereby
Thy self the worse, and so the distance greater.
Be not thine own worm. Yet such jealousy
As hurts not others, but may make thee better,
Is a good spur. Correct thy passions' spite;
Then may the beasts draw thee to happy light.

XLV

When baseness is exalted, do not bate
The place its honor for the person's sake.
The shrine is that which thou dost venerate,
And not the beast that bears it on his back.
I care not though the cloth of state should be
Not of rich arras, but mean tapestry.

XLVI

Thy friend put in thy bosom; wear his eyes
Still in thy heart that he may see what's there.
If cause require, thou art his sacrifice;
Thy drops of blood must pay down all his fear.
But love is lost, the way of friendship's gone,
Though David had his Jonathariy Christ his John.

XLVII

Yet be not surety if thou be a father.
Love is a personal debt. I cannot give
My children's right, nor ought he take it. Rather
Both friends should die then hinder them to live.
Fathers first enter bonds to nature's ends,
And are her sureties ere they are a friend's.

XLVIII

If thou be single, all thy goods and ground
Submit to love; but yet not more then all.
Give one estate, as one life. None is bound
To work for two, who brought himself to thrall.
God made me one man; love makes me no more,
Till labor come and make my weakness score.

XLIX

In thy discourse, if thou desire to please,
All such is courteous, useful, new, or witty.
Usefulness comes by labor, wit by ease,

Courtesy grows in court, news in the city.
Get a good stock of these, then draw the card
That suites him best of whom thy speech is heard.

L

Entice all neatly to what they know Lest;
For so thou dost thy self and him a pleasure.
But a proud ignorance will lose his rest
Rather then shew his cards. Steal from his treasure
What to ask further. Doubts well raised do lock
The speaker to thee and preserve thy stock.

LI

If thou be Master-gunner, spend not all
That thou canst speak at once; but husband it,
And give men turns of speech. Do not forestall
By lavishness thine own and others' wit.
As if thou maddest thy will. A civil guest
Will no more talk all, then eat all, the feast.

LII

Be calm in arguing; for fierceness makes
Error a fault, and truth discourtesy.
Why should I feel another man's mistakes
More than his sicknesses or poverty
In love I should; but anger is not love,
Nor wisdom neither. Therefore gently move.

LIII

Calmness is great advantage. He that lets
Another chafe may warm him at his fire,
Mark all his wandering, and enjoy his frets;
As cunning fencers suffer heat to tire.
Truth dwells not in the clouds; the bow that's there
Doth often aim at, never hit the sphere.

LIV

Mark what another says; for many are
Full of themselves and answer their own notion.
Take all into thee; then with equal care
Balance each dream of reason, like a potion.
If truth be with thy friend, be with them both;
Share in the conquest and confess a troth.

LV

Be useful where thou live, that they may
Both want and wish thy pleasing presence still.
Kindness, good parts, great places are the way
To compass this. Find out men's wants and will,
And meet them there. All worldly joys go less
To the one joy of doing kindnesses.

LVI

Pitch thy behavior low, thy projects high;
So shalt thou humble and magnanimous be.
Sink not in spirit. Who aim at the sky
Shoots higher much then he that means a tree.
A grain of glory mixt with humbleness
Cures both a fever and lethargicness.

LVII

Let thy mind still be bent still plotting where,
And when, and how the business may be done.
Slackness breeds worms; but the sure traveler.
Though he alight sometimes, still go on.
Active and stirring spirits live alone.
Write on the others. Here lies such a one.

LVIII

Slight not the smallest loss, whether it be
In love or honor, take account of all.

Shine like the sun in every corner.

Whether thy stock of credit swell or fall.

Who say, I care not, those I give for lost;

And to instruct them, it will not quit the cost.

LIX

Scorn no man's love, though of a mean degree;

(Love is a present for a mighty king)

Much less make any one thine enemy.

As guns destroy, so may a little sling.

The cunning workman never doth refuse

The meanest tool that he may chance to use.

LX

All foreign wisdom doth amount to this,

To take all that is given: whether wealth,

Or love, or language; nothing comes amiss.

A good digestion turn all to health.

And then as far as fair behavior may,

Strike off all scores; none are so clear as they.

LXI .

Keep all thy native good and naturalize

All foreign of that name, but scorn their ill:

Embrace their activeness, not vanities.

Who follows all things forfeit his will.

If thou observe strangers in each fit,

In time they'll run thee out of all thy wit.

LXII

Affect in things about thee cleanliness,

That all may gladly board thee, as a flower.

Slovens take up their stock of noisomness

Beforehand, and anticipate their last hour.

Let thy mind's sweetness have his operation

Upon thy body, clothes, and habitation.

LXIII

In Almes regard thy means and others' merit.

Think heaven a better bargain then to give

Only thy single market-money for it.

Join hands with God to make a man to live.

Give to all something; to a good poor man.

Till thou change names and be where he began.

LXIV

Man is God*s image, but a poor man is

Christ's stamp to boot; both images regard.

God reckons for him, counts the favor his.

Write, So much given to God; thou shalt be heard.

Let thy alms go before and keep heaven's gate

Open for thee, or both may come too late.

LXV

Restore to God his due in tithe and time.

A tithe purloined cankers the whole estate.

Sundays observe: think when the bells do chime,

'T is angels' music; therefore come not late.

God then deals blessings. If a king did so,

Who would not haste, nay give, to see the show?

LXVI

Twice on the day his due is understood;

For all the week thy food so oft he gave thee.

Thy cheer is mended; bate not of the food

Because it is better, and perhaps may save thee.

Thwart not the Almighty God. O be not cross!

Fast when thou wilt; but then it is gain, not loss.

LXVII

Though private prayer be a brave design,

Yet public hath more promises, more love;

And love's a weight to hearts, to eyes a sign.

We all are but cold suitors; let us move

Where it is warmest. Leave thy six and seven;

Pray with the most: for where most pray is heaven.

LXVIII

When once thy foot enters the church, be bare.

God is more there then thou for thou art there

Only by his permission. Then beware,

And make thy self all reverence and fear.

Kneeling near spoiled silk stocking. Quit thy state.

All equal are within the churches gate.

LXIX

Resort to sermons, but to prayers most:

Praying's the end of preaching. O be dearest,

Stay not for the other pin. Why thou hast lost

A joy for it worth worlds. Thus hell doth jest

Away thy blessings, and extremely flout thee;

Thy clothes being fast, but thy soul loose about thee.

LXX

In time of service seal up both thine eyes,

And send them to thine heart; that spying sin.

They may weep out the stains by them did rise.

Those doors being shut, all by the ear comes in.

Who marks in church-time others' symmetric,

Makes all their beauty his deformity.

LXXI

Let vain or busy thoughts have there no part:

Bring not thy plough, thy plots, thy pleasures thither.

Christ purged his temple; so must thou thy heart.

All worldly thoughts are but thieves met together

To cousin thee. Look to thy actions well:

For churches are either our heaven or hell.

LXXII

Judge not the preacher; for he is thy Judge.

If thou mistake him, thou conceive him not.

God call preaching folly. Do not grudge

To pick out treasures from an earthen pot.

The worst speak something good; if all want sense,

God takes a text and preach patience.

LXXIII

He that gets patience, and the blessing which

Preachers conclude with, hath not lost his pains.

He that by being at church escapes the ditch,

Which he might fall in by companions, gains.

He that loves God's abode, and to combine

With saints on earth, shall one day with them shine.

LXXIV

Jest not at preachers' language or expression.

How know thou but thy sins made him miscarry?

Then turn thy faults and his into confession.

God sent him, whatsoever he be. O tarry.

And love him for his Master. His condition.

Though it be ill, makes him no ill Physician.

LXXV

None shall in hell such bitter pangs endure,

As those who mock at God's way of salvation.

Whom oil and balsam kill, what salve can cure?

They drink with greediness a full damnation.

The Jews refused thunder; and we, folly.

Though God do hedge us in, yet who is holy.

LXXVI

Sum up at night what thou hast done by day;

And in the morning, what thou hast to do.

Dress and undress thy soul: mark the decay

And growth of it; if with thy watch, that too

Be down, then wind up both. Since we shall be

Most surely judged, make thy accounts agree.

LXXVII

In brief, acquit thee bravely; play the man.

Look not on pleasures as they come, but go.

Defer not the least virtue. Life's poor span

Make not an ell by trifling in thy we.

If thou do ill, the joy fades, not the pains:

If well, the pain doth fade, the joy remains.

II.THE RESOLVE

TWO SONNETS

TO HIS MOTHER

I (1610)

My God, where is that ancient heat towards thee

Wherewith whole shoals of Martyrs once did burn,

Besides their other flames? Doth Poetry

Wear Venus' livery, only serve her turn?

Why are not Sonnets made of thee, and lays

Upon thine Altar burnt? Cannot thy love

Heighten a spirit to sound out thy praise
As well as any she? Cannot thy Dove
Outstrip their Cupid easily in flight?
Or, since thy ways are deep and still the same,
Will not verse run smooth that bears thy name?
Why doth that fire, which by thy power and might
Each breast does feel, no braver fuel choose
Than that which one day Worms may chance refuse?

II

Sure, Lord, there is enough in thee to dry
Oceans of Ink; for as the Deluge did
Cover the Earth, so doth thy Majesty;
Each cloud distils thy praise, and doth forbid
Poets to turn it to another use.
Roses and Lilies speak thee; and to make
A pair of Cheeks of them, is thy abuse.
Why should I Women's eyes for Chrystal take?
Such poor invention burns in their low mind
Whose fire is wild, and doth not upward go
To praise, and on thee, Lord, some ink bestow.
Open the bones, and you shall nothing find
In the best face but filth; when Lord, in Thee
The beauty lies in the discovery.

LOVE

I

Immortal Love, author of this great frame.
Sprung from that beauty which can never fade,
How hath man parceled out thy glorious name
And thrown it on that dust which thou hast made.
While mortal love doth all the title gain!

Which siding with invention, they together

Bear all the sway, possessing heart and brain,

(Thy workmanship) and give thee share in neither.

Wit fancies beauty, beauty raise wit.

The world is theirs; they two play out the game.

Thou standing by. And though thy glorious name

Wrought our deliverance from the infernal pit,

Who sings thy praise? Only a scarf or glove

Doth warm our hands and make them write of love.

II

Immortal Heat, O let thy greater flame

Attract the lesser to it! Let those fires.

Which shall consume the world, first make it tame,

And kindle in our hearts such true desires

As may consume our lusts and make thee way.

Then shall our hearts pant thee; then shall our brain

All her invention on thine Altar lay.

And there in hymns send back thy fire again.

Our eyes shall see thee, which before saw dust,

Dust blown by with till that they both were blind.

Thou shalt recover all thy goods in kind,

Who wert disseized by usurping lust.

All knees shall bow to thee; all wit shall rise

And praise him who did make and mend our eyes.

JORDAN

Who says that fictions only and false hair

Become a verse? Is there in truth no beauty?

Is all good structure in a winding stair?

May no lines pass except they do their duty

Not to a true, but painted chair?

Is it no verse except enchanted groves

And sudden arbors shadow course-spun lines?

Must purling streams refresh a lover's loves?

Must all be veiled, while he that reads divines,

Catching the sense at two removes?

Shepherds are honest people; let them sing,

Riddle who list for me, and pull for Prime.

I envy no man's nightingale or spring;

Nor let them punish me with loss of rhyme,

Who plainly say, My God, My King,

JORDAN

When first my lines of heavenly joys made mention,

Such was their luster, they did so excel,

That I sought out quaint words and trim invention;

My thoughts began to burnish, sprout, and swell,

Curling with metaphors a plain intention,

Decking the sense as if it were to sell.

Thousands of notions in my brain did run,

Offspring their service, if I were not sped.

I often blotted what I had begun;

This was not quick enough, and that was dead.

Nothing could seem too rich to clothe the sun,

Much less those joys which trample on his head.

As flames do work and wind when they ascend.

So did I weave myself into the sense.

But while I bustled, I might hear a friend

Whisper, How wide is all this long pretense I

There is in love a sweetness ready penned;

Copy out only that, and save expense.

PRAISE

To write a verse or two is all the praise

That I can raise.

Mend my estate in any ways,

Thou shalt have more.

I go to Church; help me to wings, and I

Will thither fly.

Or, if I mount unto the sky,

I will do more.

Man is all weakness; there is no such thing

As Prince or King.

His arm is short, yet with a sling

He may do more.

An herb distilled, and drunk, may dwell next door

On the same floor

To a brave soul. Exalt the poor,

They can do more.

O raise me then! Poor bees, that work all day,

Sting my delay;

Who have a work as well as they.

And much, much more.

THE QUIDDITIE

My God, a verse is not a crown,

No point of honor, or gay suit,

No hawk, or banquet, or renown,

Nor a good sword, nor yet a lute:

It cannot vault, or dance, or play;

It never was in France or Spain;

Nor can it entertain the day

With a great stable or domain.

It is no office, art, or news.

Nor the Exchange, or busy Hall.

But it is that which while I use

I am with thee; and Mostly take all.

THE ELIXER

Teach me, my God and King,

In all things thee to see;

And what I do in anything.

To do it as for thee.

Not rudely, as a beast,

To run into an action;

But still to make thee pre-pose,

And give it his perfection.

A man that looks on glass

On it may stay his eye,

Or if he please, through it pass,

And then the heaven's spy.

All may of thee partake;

Nothing can be so mean

Which with his tincture (for thy sake)

Will not grow bright and clean.

A servant with this clause

Makes drudgery divine;

Who sweeps a room, as for thy laws.

Makes that and the action fine.

This is the famous stone

That turn all to gold;

For that which God doth touch and own

Cannot for less be told.

EMPLOYMENT

He that is weary, let him sit!

My soul would stir

And trade in courtesies and wit,

Quitting the fur

To cold complexions needing it.

Man is no star, but a quick coal
Of mortal fire;
Who blows it not, nor doth control
A faint desire,
Let's his own ashes choke his soul.
When the elements did for place contest
With him whose will
Ordained the highest to be best,
The earth sat still,
And by the others is oppressed.

Life is a business, not good cheer,
Ever in wares.
The sun still shine there or here,
Whereas the stars
Watch an advantage to appear.
Oh that I were an Orange-tree,
That busy plant!
Then should I ever laden be.
And never want
Some fruit for him that dressed me.
But we are still too young or old;
The man is gone
Before we do our wares unfold.
So we freeze on,
Until the grave increase our cold.

III. THE CHURCH

SUPERLIMINARE

Thou, whom the former precepts have
Sprinkled and taught how to behave
Thy self in church, approach, and taste
The churches mystical repast.
Avoid, profaneness! Come not here!
Nothing but holy, pure, and clear,
Or that which groan to be so,
May at his peril further go.

THE SACRIFICE

Oh all ye who pass by, whose eyes and mind
To worldly things are sharp, but to me blind,
To me who took eyes that I might you find.
Was ever grief like mine?
The Princes of my people make a head
Against their Maker; they do wish me dead,
Who cannot wish except I give them bread.
Was ever grief like mine?
Without me each one who doth now me brave
Had to this day been an Egyptian slave.
They use that power against me which I gave.
Was ever grief like mine?
Mine own Apostle, who the bag did bear,
Though he had all I had, did not forbear

To sell me also and to put me there.

Was ever grief, &c.

For thirty pence he did my death devise

Who at three hundred did the ointment prize,

Not half so sweet as my sweet sacrifice.

Was ever grief like mine?

Therefore my soul melts, and my heart's dear treasure

Drops blood (the only beads) my words to measure:

O let this cup pass, if it he thy pleasure.

Was ever grief, &c.

These drops, being tempered with a sinner's tears,

A Balsome are for both the Hemispheres;

Curing all wounds but mine, all but my fears.

Was ever grief, &c.

Yet my Disciples sleep. I cannot gain

One hour of watching; but their drowsy brain

Comforts not me, and doth my doctrine stain.

Was ever grief, &;c.

Arise, arise! They come. Look, how they run I

Alas! What haste they make to be undone!

How with their lanterns do they seek the sun!

Was ever grief, &c.

With clubs and staves they seek me as a thief

Who am the way of truth, the true relief.

Most true to those who are my greatest grief.

Was ever grief like mine?

Judas, dost thou betray me with a kiss?

Canst thou find hell about my lips? And miss

Of life just at the gates of life and bliss?

Was ever grief, &c.

See, they lay hold on me not with the hands

Of faith, but fury. Yet at their commands
I suffer binding, who have loosed their bands.
Was ever grief, &c.

All my Disciples fly; fear puts a bare
Betwixt my friends and me. They leave the star
That brought the wise men of the East from far.
Was ever grief, &c.

Then from one ruler to another bound
They lead me, urging that it was not sound
What I taught. Comments would the text confound.
Was ever grief, &c.

The Priest and rulers all false witness seek
Against him who seeks not life, but is the meek
And ready Paschal Lamb of this great week.
Was ever grief like mine

Then they accuse me of great blasphemy,
That I did thrust into the Deity,
Who never thought that any robbery.
Was ever grief, &c.

Some said that I the Temple to the floor
In three days razed, and raised as before.
Why, he that built the world can do much more.
Was ever grief, &c.

Then they condemn me all with that same breath
Which I do give them daily, unto death.
Thus Adam my first breathing render.
Was ever grief, &c.

They bind, and lead me unto Herod. He
Sends me to Pilate. This makes them agree;
But yet their friendship is my enmity.
Was ever grief, &c.

Herod and all his bands do set me light
Who teach all hands to ware, fingers to fight,
And only am the Lord of hosts and might.

       Was ever grief like mine?

Herod in judgment sits, while I do stand;
Examines me with a censorious hand.
I him obey, who all things else command.

       Was ever grief, &c.

The Jews accuse me with despitefulness,
And vying malice with my gentleness.
Pick quarrels with their only happiness.

       Was ever grief, &c.

I answer nothing, but with patience prove
If stone hearts will melt with gentle love.
But who does hawk at eagles with a dove?

       Was ever grief, &c.

My silence rather doth augment their cry;
My dove doth back into my bosom fly.
Because the raging waters still are high.

       Was ever grief, &c.

Hear how they cry aloud still, Crucify I
It is not fit he live a day, they cry.
Who cannot live less then eternally.

       Was ever grief like mine?

Pilate, a stranger, hold off; but they,
Mine own dear people, cry. Away, away!
With noises confused fighting the day.

       Was ever grief, &c.

Yet still they shout and cry and stop their ears.
Putting my life among their sins and fears.
And therefore with my blood on them and theirs.

Was ever grief, &c.

See how spite cankers things. These words, aright

Used and wished, are the whole world's light;

But honey is their gall, brightness their night.

Was ever grief, &c.

They choose a murderer, and all agree

In him to do themselves a courtesy;

For it was their own cause who killed me.

Was ever grief, &c.

And a seditious murderer he was,

But I the Prince of peace; peace that doth pass

All understanding, more than heaven doth glass.

Was ever grief like mine?

Why, Cesar is their only King, not I.

He clave the stony rock when they were dry;

But surely not their hearts, as I well try.

Was ever grief, &c.

Ah, How they scourge me! Yet my tenderness

Doubles each lash, and yet their bitterness

Winds up my grief to a mysteriousness.

Was ever grief, &c.

They buffet me and box me as they list,

Who grasp the earth and heaven with my fist,

And never yet, whom I would punish, missed.

Was ever grief, &c.

Behold, they spit on me in scornful wise

Who by my spittle gave the blind man eyes.

Leaving his blindness to mine enemies.

Was ever grief, &c.

My face they cover, though it be divine.

As Closes' face was vailed, so is mine,

xxx

Lest on their double-dark souls either shine.
Was ever grief like mine?
Servants and objects flout me; they are witty:
Now prophesy who strikes thee, is their ditty.
So they in me deny themselves all pity.
Was ever grief, &c.
And now I am delivered unto death,
Which each one calls for so with utmost breath
That he before me well nigh suffer.
Was ever grief, &c.
Weep not, dear friends, since I for both have wept
When all my tears were blood, the while you slept.
Your tears for your own fortunes should be kept.
Was ever grief, &c.
The soldiers lead me to the common hall;
There they deride me, they abuse me all.
Yet for twelve heavenly legions I could call.
Was ever grief, &c.
Then with a scarlet robe they me array;
Which shews my blood to be the only way
And cordial left to repair man's decay.
Was ever grief like mine?
Then on my head a crown of thorns I wear;
For these are all the grapes Sion doth bear,
Though I my vine planted and watered there.
Was ever grief, &c.
So sits the earth's great curse in Adam's fall
Upon my head. So I remove it all
From the' earth unto my brows, and bear the thrall.
Was ever grief, &c.
Then with the reed they gave to me before

They strike my head, the rock from whence all store

Of heavenly blessings issue evermore.

Was ever grief, &c.

They bow their knees to me and cry, Hail king!

Whatever scoffs or scornfulness can bring,

I am the floor, the sink, where they it fling.

Was ever grief, &c.

Yet since man's scepters are as frail as reeds,

And thorny all their crowns, blondie their weeds,

I, who am Truth, turn into truth their deeds.

Was ever grief like mine?

The soldiers also spit upon that face

Which Angels did desire to have the grace,

And Prophets, once to see, but found no place.

Was ever grief, &c.

Thus trimmed, forth they bring me to the rout,

Who Crucify him! cry with one strong shout.

God holds his peace at man, and man cries out.

Was ever grief, &c.

They lead me in once more, and putting then

Mine own clothes on, they leady me out again.

Whom devils fly, thus is he tossed of men.

Was ever grief, &c.

And now weary of sport, glad to engross

All spite in one, counting my life their loss.

They carry me to my most bitter cross.

Was ever grief, &c.

My cross I bear myself until I faint.

Then Simon bears it for me by constraint,

The decreed burden of each mortal Saint.

Was ever grief like mine?

O all ye who pass by, behold and see I
Man stole the fruit, but I must climb the tree;
The tree of life to all but only me.
Was ever grief, &c.
Lo, here I hang, charged with a world of sin.
The greater world of the two; for that came in
By words, but this by sorrow I must win.
Was ever grief, &c.
Such sorrow as, if sinful man could feel
Or feel his part, he would not cease to kneel
Till all were melted, though he were all steel.
Was ever grief, &c.

But, O my God, my God I why leave thou me.
The Son, in whom thou dost delight to be?
My God, my God
Never was grief like mine.
Shame tears my soul, my body many a wound;
Sharp nails pierce this, but sharper that confound;
Reproches, which are free, while I am bound.
Was ever grief like mine?
Now heal thy self. Physician, now come down I
Alas! I did so, when I left my crown
And father's smile for you, to feel his frown.
Was ever grief, &c.
In healing not myself, there doth consist
All that salvation which ye now resist;
Your safety in my sickness doth subsist.
Was ever grief, &c.
Betwixt two thieves I spend my utmost breath.
As he that for some robbery suffer.

Alas! what have I stolen from you? Death.

Was ever grief, &c.

A king my title is, prefix on high;

Yet by my subjects am condemned to die

A servile death in servile company.

Was ever grief, &c.

They gave me vinegar mingled with gall,

But more with malice. Yet when they did call.

With Manna, Angels' food, I fed them all.

Was ever grief like mine?

They part my garments and by lot dispose

My coat, the type of love, which once cured those

Who sought for help, never malicious foes.

Was ever grief, &c.

Nay, after death their spite shall further go;

For they will pierce my side, I full well know,

That as sin came, so Sacraments might flow.

Was ever grief, &c.

But now I die, now all is finished;

My we, man's weal. And now I bow my head.

Only let others say, when I am dead,

Never was grief like mine.

GOOD FRIDAY

O My chief good,

How shall I measure out thy blood?

How shall I count what thee befell,

And each grief tell?

Shall I thy woes

Number according to thy foes

Or, since one star showed thy first breath,

Shall all thy death?

Or shall each leaf

Which falls in Autumn score a grief?

Or cannot leaves, but fruit, be sign

Of the true vine?

Then let each hour

Of my whole life one grief devour;

That thy distress through all may run,

And be my sun.

Or rather let

My several sins their sorrows get;

That as each beast his cure doth know.

Each sin may so.

Since blood is fittest, Lord, to write

Thy sorrows in and bloody fight;

My heart hath store, write there, where in

One box doth he both ink and sin.

That when sin spies so many foes,

Thy whips, thy nails, thy wounds, thy woes.

All come to lodge there, sin may say,

No room for me, and fly away.

Sin being gone, oh fill the place

And keep possession with thy grace!

Lest sin take courage and return,

And all the writings blot or burn.

EASTER

Rise, heart, thy Lord is risen. Sing his praise

Without delays.

Who takes thee by the hand, that thou likewise

With him may rise;

That, as his death called thee to dust,

His life may make thee gold, and much more, just.

Awake, my lute, and struggle for thy part
With all thy art:
The cross taught all wood to resound his name
Who bore the same;
His stretched sinews taught all strings what key
Is best to celebrate this most high day.
Consort both heart and lute, and twist a song
Pleasant and long.
Or, since all music is but three parts vied
And multiplied,
O let thy blessed Spirit bear a part.
And make up our defects with his sweet art.

got me flowers to straw thy way,
I got me boughs off many a tree,
But thou was up by break of day.
And brought thy sweets along with thee.
The Sun arising in the East,
Though he give light, and the East perfume.
If they should offer to contest
With thy arising, they presume.
Can there be any day but this.
Though many suns to shine endeavor?
We count three hundred, but we miss;
There is but one, and that one ever.

WHITSUNDAY

Listen, sweet Dove, unto my song
And spread thy golden wings in me;
Hatching my tender heart so long
Till it get wing and fly away with thee.
Where is that fire which once descended
On thy Apostles? Thou didst then

Keep open house, richly attended.

Feasting all comers by twelve chosen men.

Such glorious gifts thou didst bestow

That the earth did like a heaven appear;

The stars were coming down to know

If they might mend their wages and serve here.

The sun, which once did shine alone,

Hung down his head and wished for night

When he beheld twelve suns for one

Going about the world and giving light.

But since those pipes of gold, which brought

That cordial water to our ground.

Were cut and martyred by the fault

Of those who did themselves through their side wound,

Thou shut the door and keep within,

Scarce a good joy creeps through the chink;

And if the braves of conquering since

Did not excite thee, we should wholly sink.

Lord, though we change, thou art the same;

The same sweet God of love and light.

Restore this day, for thy great name,

Unto his ancient and miraculous right.

TRINITY-SUNDAY

Lord, who hast formed me out of mud,

And hast redeemed me through thy blood.

And sanctified me to do good.

Purge all my sins done heretofore;

For I confess my heavy score,

And I will strive to sin no more.

Enrich my heart, mouth, hands in me.

With faith, with hope, with charity.

That I may run, rise, rest with thee.

TO ALL ANGELS AND SAINTS

Oh glorious spirits, who after all your bands

See the smooth face of God without a frown

Or strict commands;

Where everyone is king, and hath his crown

If not upon his head, yet in his hands;

Not out of envy or maliciousness

Do I forbear to crave your special aid.

I would address

My vows to thee most gladly, blessed Maid,

And Mother of my God, in my distress.

Thou art the holy mine whence came the gold,

The great restorative for all decay

In young and old.

Thou art the cabinet where the Jewell lay;

Chiefly to thee would I my soul unfold.

CHRISTMAS

All after pleasures as I rid one day,

My horse and I both tired, body and mind,

With full cry of affections quite astray,

I took up in the next is I could find.

There when I came, whom found I but my dear.

My dearest Lord, expecting till the grief

Of pleasures brought me to him, ready there

To be all passengers' most sweet relief?

O Thou, whose glorious yet contracted light.

Wrapped in night's mantle, stole into a manger.

Since my dark soul and brutish is thy right,

To Man of all beasts be not thou a stranger.

Furnish and deck my soul, that thou may have

A better lodging then a rack, or grave.

The shepherds sing, and shall I silent be?

My God, no hymn for thee?

My soul's a shepherd too; a flock it feeds

Of thoughts, and words, and deeds.

The pasture is thy word; the streams, thy grace

Enriching all the place.

Shepherd and flock shall sing, and all my powers

Out-sing the day-light hours.

Then we will cud the sun for letting night

Take up his place and right.

We sing one common Lord; wherefore he should

Himself the candle hold.

I will go searching, till I find a sun

Shall stay till we have done,

A willing shiner, that shall shine as gladly

As frost-nipped suns look sadly.

Then we will sing and shine all our own day,

And one another pay.

His beams shall cheer my breast, and both so twine

Till even his beams sing and my music shine.

LENT

Welcome, dear feast of Lent! Who loves not thee.

He loves not Temperance or Authority,

But is composed of passion.

The Scriptures bid us fast; the Church says, now;

Give to thy Mother what thou wouldst allow

To every Corporation.

The humble soul, composed of love and fear.

Begins at home and lays the burden there,

When doctrines disagree.

He says, in things which use hath justly got,
I am a scandal to the Church, and not
The Church is so to me.
True Christians should be glad of an occasion
To use their temperance, seeking no evasion
When good is seasonable;
Unless Authority which should increase
The obligation in us, make it less,
And Power itself disable.
Besides the cleanness of sweet abstinence,
Quick thoughts and motions at a small expense,
A face not fearing light;
Whereas in fullness there are sluttish fumes,
Soar exhalations, and dishonest rhymes.
Revenging the delight.
Then those same pendant profits, which the spring
And Easter intimate, enlarge the thing
And goodness of the deed.
Neither ought other men's abuse of Lent
Spoil the good use, lest by that argument
We forfeit all our Creed.
It's true we cannot reach Christ's fortieth day;
Yet to go part of that religious way
Is better then to rest.
We cannot reach our Savior's purity;
Yet are we bid, Be holy even as he.
In both let's do our best.
Who go in the way which Christ hath gone,
Is much more sure to meet with him then one
That travel by-ways.
Perhaps my God, though he be far before,

May turn and take me by the hand, and more

May strengthen my decays.

Yet Lord instruct us to improve our fast

By starving sin, and taking such repast

As may our faults control;

That every man may revel at his door.

Not in his parlor; banqueting the poor.

And among those his soul.

SUNDAY

O day most calm, most bright,

The fruit of this, the next world's bud,

The indorsement of supreme delight.

Writ by a friend, and with his blood;

The couch of time, care's balm and bay;

The week were dark but for thy light.

Thy torch doth show the way.

The other days and thou

Make up one man, whose face thou art.

Knocking at heaven with thy brow.

The work-days are the back-part;

The burden of the week lies there.

Making the whole to stoup and bow

Till thy release appear.

Man had straight forward gone

To endless death; but thou dost pull

And turn us round to look on one

Whom, if we were not very dull,

We could not choose but look on still;

Since there is no place so alone

The which he doth not fill.

Sundays the pillars are

On which heavens palace arched lies;
The other days fill up the spare
And hollow room with vanities.
They are the fruitful beds and borders
In God's rich garden: that is bare
Which parts their ranks and orders.
The Sundays of man's life,
Thredded together on time's string,
Make bracelets to adorn the wife
Of the eternal glorious King.
On Sunday heaven's gate stands off.
Blessings are plentiful and rife.
More plentiful then hope.
This day my Savior rose.
And did enclose this light for his;
That, as each beast his manger knows,
Man might not of his fodder miss.
Christ hath took in this piece of ground,
And made a garden there for those
Who want herbs for their wound.
The rest of our Creation
Our great Redeemer did remove
With the same shake which at his passion
Did the earth and all things with it move.
As Samson bore the doors away,
Christ's hands, though nailed, wrought our salvation
And did unhinge that day.
The brightness of that day
We sullied by our foul offence;
Wherefore that robe we cast away.
Having a new at his expense

Whose drops of blood paid the full price

That was required to make us gay,

And fit for Paradise.

Thou art a day of mirth;

And where the week-days trail on ground.

Thy flight is higher, as thy birth.

O let me take thee at the bound,

Leaping with thee from seven to seven.

Till that we both, being tossed from earth,

Fly hand in hand to heaven!

PRAYER

Prayer the Churches banquet, Angel's age,

God's breath in man returning to his birth,

The soul in paraphrase, heart in pilgrimage.

The Christian plummet sounding heaven and earth;

Engine against the Almighty, sinner's owe,

Reversed thunder, Christ-side-piercing spear,

The six-days-world transposing in an hour,

A kind of tune which all things hear and fear;

Softness and peace and joy and love and bliss,

Exalted Manna, gladness of the best,

Heaven in ordinary, man well dress.

The milky way, the bird of Paradise,

Church-bels beyond the stars heard, the soul's blood.

The land of spices; something understood.

THE H. SCRIPTURES

I

Oh Book! Infinite sweetness! Let my heart

Suck every letter and a honey gain,

Precious for any grief in any part.

To clear the breast, to mollify all pain.

Thou art all health, health thriving till it make
A full eternity. Thou art a mass
Of strange delights, where we may wish and take.
Ladies, look here! This is the thankful glass
That mends the looker's eyes; this is the well
That washes what it shows. Who can endear
Thy praise too much? Thou art heaven's Lidger here,
Working against the states of death and hell.
Thou art joys hand sell. Heaven lies flat in thee,
Subject to every mounter's bended knee.

II

Oh that I knew how all thy lights combine,
And the configurations of their glory!
Seeing not only how each verse doth shine,
But all the constellations of the story.
This verse marks that, and both do make a motion
Unto a third, that ten leaves off doth lie;
Then as dispersed herbs do watch a potion,
These three make up some Christian's destiny.
Such are thy secrets, which my life makes good.
And comments on thee; for in everything
Thy words do find me out, and parallels bring,
And in another make me understood.
Stares are poor books, and oftentimes do miss;
This book of stares lights to eternal bliss.

H. BAPTISM

As he that sees a dark and shady grove
Stays not, but looks beyond it on the sky;
So when I view my sins, mine eyes remove
More backward still and to that water fly
Which is above the heavens, whose spring and rent

Is in my dear Redeemer's pierced side.

O blessed streams! Either ye do prevent

And stop our sins from growing thick and wide.

Or else give tears to drown them as they grow.

In you Redemption measures all my time

And spreads the plaster equal to the crime.

You taught the book of life my name, that so,

Whatever future sins should me miscall,

Your first acquaintance might discredit all.

THE H. COMMUNION

Not in rich furniture or fine array,

Nor in a wedge of gold,

Thou, who from me was sold,

To me dost now thy self-convey;

For so thou shouldn't without me still have been,

Leaving within me sin.

But by the way of nourishment and strength

Thou creep into my breast.

Making thy way my rest.

And thy small quantities my length;

Which spread their forces into every part.

Meeting sin's force and art.

Yet can these not get over to my soul,

Leaping the wall that parts

Our souls and fleshly hearts;

But as the outworks, they may control

My rebel-flesh, and carrying thy name.

Affright both sin and shame.

Only thy grace, which with these elements comes,

Know the ready way

And hath the privy key,

Opening the soul's most sub-tile rooms;

While those to spirits refined at door attend

Dispatches from their friend.

Give me my captive soul, or take

My body also thither.

Another lift like this will make

Them both to be together.

Before that sin turned flesh to stone.

And all our lump to leaven,

A fervent sigh might well have blown

Our innocent earth to heaven.

For sure when Adam did not know

To sin, or sin to smother,

He might to heaven from Paradise go

As from one room to another.

Thou hast restored us to this ease

By this thy heavenly blood;

Which I can go to when I please.

And leave the earth to their food.

CHURCH-MUSIC

Sweetest of sweets, I thank you! When displeasure

Did through my body wound my mind,

You took me thence, and in your house of pleasure

A dainty lodging me assigned.

Now I in you without a body move,

Rising and falling with your wings.

We both together sweetly live and love.

Yet say sometimes, God help poor Kings.

Comfort, I'll die; for if you poste from me,

Sure I shall do so, and much more.

But if I travel in your company.

You know the way to heaven's door.

CHURCH-MONUMENTS

While that my soul repairs to her devotion,
Here I entomb my flesh, that it betimes
May take acquaintance of this heap of dust.
To which the blast of death's incessant motion,
Fed with the exhalation of our crimes,
Drives all at last. Therefore I gladly trust
My body to this school, that it may learn
To spell his elements, and find his birth
Written in dusty heraldry and lines
Which dissolution sure doth best discern,
Comparing dust with dust, and earth with earth.
These laugh at least and Marble put for signs
To sever the good fellowship of dust.
And spoil the meeting. What shall point out them.
When they shall bow and kneel and fall down flat
To kiss those heaps which now they have in trust?
Dear flesh, while I do pray, learn here thy stemmed
And true descent; that when thou shalt grow fat
And wanton in thy cravings, thou may know
That flesh is but the glass which holds the dust
That measures all our time; which also shall
Be crumbled into dust. Mark here below
How tame these ashes are, how free from lust,
That thou may fit thyself against thy fall.

IV.MEDITATION

CHARMS AND KNOTS

Who read a chapter when they rise,

Shall near be troubled with ill eyes.

A poor man's rod, when thou dost ride,

Is both a weapon and a guide.

Who shuts his hand, hath lost his gold;

Who opens it, hath it twice told.

Who goes to bed and doth not pray,

Make two nights to every day.

Who by aspersions throw a stone

At the head of others, hit their own.

Who looks on ground with humble eyes,

Finds himself there, and seeks to rise.

When the hair is sweet through pride or lust.

The powder doth forget the dust.

Take one from ten, and what remains?

Ten still, if sermons go for gains.

In shallow waters heaven doth show;

But who drinks on, to hell may go.

MAN

My God, I heard this day

That none doth build a stately habitation

But he that means to dwell therein.

What house more stately hath there been,

Or can be, then is Man? To whose creation

All things are in decay.

For Man is everything,

And more. He is a tree, yet bears no fruit;

A beast, yet is, or should be more;

Reason and speech we only bring.

Parrats may thank us if they are not mute,

They go upon the score.

Man is all symmetry,

Full of proportions, one limb to another,
And all to all the world besides.
Each part may call the farthest, brother;
For head with foot hath private amity.
And both with moons and tides.

Nothing hath got so far
But Man hath caught and kept it as his prey.
His eyes dismount the highest stare.
He is in little all the sphere.
Herbs gladly cure our flesh, because that they
Find their acquaintance there.

For us the winds do blow,
The earth doth rest, heaven move, and fountains flow.
Nothing we see but means our good.
As our delight, or as our treasure;
The whole is either our cupboard of food
Or cabinet of pleasure.

The stares have us to bed;
Night draws the curtain, which the sun withdraws;
Music and light attend our head.
All things unto our flesh are kind
In their descent and being; to our mind
In their ascent and cause.

Each thing is full of duty:
Waters united are our navigation;
Distinguished, our habitation;
Below, our drink; above, our meat;
Both are our cleanliness. Hath one such beauty?
Then how are all things neat?

More servants wait on Man
Then he'll take notice of; in every path

He treads down that which doth befriend him

When sickness makes him pale and wan.

Oh mighty love! Man is one world, and hath

Another to attend him.

Since then, my God, thou hast

So brave a Palace built, O dwell in it,

That it may dwell with thee at last!

Till then afford us so much wit

That as the world serves us we may serve thee,

And both thy servants be.

THE WORLD

Love built a stately house; where Fortune came,

And spinning phans she was heard to say

That her fine cobwebs did support the frame,

Whereas they were supported by the same.

But Wisdom quickly swept them all away.

Then Pleasure came, who liking not the fashion,

Began to make Balcones, Terraces,

Till she had weakened all by alteration;

But reverend laws and many a proclamation

Reformed all at length with menaces.

Then entered Sin, and with that Sycamore,

Whose leaves first sheltered man from drought and dew,

Working and winding slyly evermore,

The inward walls and Sommers cleft and tore;

But Grace shored these, and cut that as it grew.

Then Sinne combined with Death in a firm band

To raise the building to the very floor;

Which they effected, none could them withstand.

But Love and Grace took Glory by the hand

And built a braver Palace then before.

1

FAITH

Lord, how couldn't thou so much appease
Thy wrath for sin, as when man's sight was dime
And could see little, to regard his ease
And bring by Faith all things to him?
Hungry I was and had no meat.
I did conceit a most delicious feast;
I had it straight, and did as truly eat
As ever did a welcome guest.
There is a rare outlandish root
Which, when I could not get, I thought it here;
That apprehension cured so well my foot
That I can walk to heaven well near.
I owed thousands and much more.
I did believe that I did nothing owe
And lived accordingly; my creditor
Believes so too, and lets me go.
Faith makes me anything, or all
That I believe is in the sacred story.
And where sin place me in Adam's fall.
Faith sets me higher in his glory.
If I go lower in the book,
What can be lower than the common manger?
Faith puts me there with him who sweetly took
Our flesh and frailty, death and danger.
If bliss had lien in art or strength,
None but the wise or strong had gained it.
Where now by Faith all arms are of a length;
One size doth all conditions fit.
A peasant may believe as much
As a great Clerk, and reach the highest stature.

Thus dost thou make proud knowledge bend and crouch

While grace fills up uneven nature.

When creatures had no recall light

Inherent in them, thou didst make the sun

Impute a luster and allow them bright,

And in this shew what Christ hath done.

That which before was darkened clean

With bushy groves, pricking the looker's eye,

Vanished away when Faith did change the scene;

And then appeared a glorious sky.

What though my body run to dust?

Faith cleaves unto it, counting every grain

With an exact and most particular trust,

Reserving all for flesh again.

REDEMPTION

Having been tenant long to a rich Lord,

Not thriving, I resolved to be bold.

And make a suit unto him to afford

A new small-rented lease and cancel the old.

In heaven at his manor I him sought.

They told me there that he was lately gone

About some land which he had dearly bought

Long since on earth, to take possession.

I straight returned, and knowing his great birth.

Sought him accordingly in great resorts,

In cities, theatres, gardens, parks, and courts.

At length I heard a ragged noise and mirth

Of thieves and murderers; there I him espied.

Who straight, Your suit is granted, said, and died.

HUMILITY

I saw the Virtues sitting hand in hand

In several ranks upon an azure throne,
Where all the beasts and fowls by their command
Presented tokens of submission.
Humility, who sat the lowest there
To execute their call,
When by the beasts the presents tendered were.
Gave them about to all.
The angry Lion did present his paw,
Which by consent was given to Mansuetude.
The fearful Hare her ears, which by their law
Humility did reach to Fortitude.
The jealous Turkie brought his coral-chain;
That went to Temperance.
On Justice was bestowed the Foxes brain,
Killed in the way by chance.

UNGRATEFULNESS

Lord, with what bounty and rare clemency
Hast thou redeemed us from the grave!
If thou had let us run,
Gladly had man adored the sun,
And thought his god most brave;
Where now we shall be better gods then he.
Thou hast but two rare cabinets full of treasure,
The Trinity and Incarnation.
Thou hast unlocked them both,
And made them jewels to betroth
The work of thy creation
Unto thy self in everlasting pleasure.
The statelier cabinet is the Trinity,
Whose sparkling light access denies.
Therefore thou dost not show

This fully to us till death blow

The dust into our eyes;

For by that powder thou wilt make us see.

MISERY

Lord, let the Angels praise thy name;

Man is a foolish thing, a foolish thing.

Folly and Sinne play all his game.

His house still burns, and yet he still doth sing,

Man is but grass,

He knows it, fill the glass.

How canst thou brook his foolishness?

Why he'll not lose a cup of drink for thee.

Bid him but temper his excess,

Not he; he knows where he can better be,

As he will swear,

Then to serve thee in fear.

What strange pollutions doth he wed.

And make his own! As if none knew but he.

No man shall beat into his head

That thou within his curtains drawn canst see.

They are of cloth,

Where never yet came moth.

Man cannot serve thee; let him go,

And serve the swine. There, there is his delight.

He doth not like this virtue, no;

Give him his dirt to wallow in all night.

These Preachers make

His head to shoot and make.

Oh foolish man! Where are thine eyes?

How hast thou lost them in a crowd of cares?

Thou pull the rug and wilt not rise.

No, not to purchase the whole pack of stars.

There let them shine.

Thou must go sleep or dine.

The bird that sees a dainty bow

Made in the tree where she was wont to sit,

Wonders and sings, but not his power

Who made the arbor; this exceeds her wit.

But Man doth know

The spring whence all things flow:

And yet, as though he knew it not,

His knowledge winks and lets his humors reign.

They make his life a constant blot.

And all the blood of God to run in vain.

Ah wretch! What verse

Can thy strange ways rehearse?

Indeed at first Man was a treasure,

A box of jewels, shop of rarities,

A ring whose pose was. My pleasure.

He was a garden in a Paradise.

Glory and grace

Did crown his heart and face.

But sin hath fooled him. Now he is

A lump of flesh, without a foot or wing

To raise him to the glimpse of bliss;

A sick tossed vessel, dashing on each thing;

Nay, his own shelf;

My God, I mean myself.

MORTIFICATION

How soon doth man decay!

When clothes are taken from a chest of sweets

To swaddle infants, whose young breath

Scarce knows the way.

Those clouts are little winding sheets

Which do consign and send them unto death.

When boys go first to bed.

They step into their voluntary graves.

Sleep binds them fast; only their breath

Makes them not dead.

Successive nights, like rolling waves,

Convey them quickly who are bound for death.

When youth is frank and free.

And calls for music while his veins do swell.

All day exchanging mirth and breath

In company.

That music summons to the knell

Which shall befriend him at the house of death.

DEATH

Death, thou was once an uncouth hideous thing,

Nothing but bones,

The sad effect of sadder groans;

Thy mouth was open but thou couldn't not sing.

For we considered thee as at some six

Or ten years hence.

After the loss of life and sense.

Flesh being turned to dust, and bones to sticks.

We look on this side of thee, shooting short;

Where we did find

The shells of fledge souls left behind.

Dry dust, which sheds no tears but may extort.

But since our Savior's death did put some blood

Into thy face.

Thou art grown fair and full of grace,

Much in request, much sought for as a good.

For we do now behold thee gay and glad.

As at dooms-day;

When souls shall wear their new array,

And all thy bones with beauty shall be clad.

Therefore we can go die as sleep, and trust

Half that we have

Unto an honest faithful grave.

Making our pillows either down or dust.

DOOMS-DAY

Come away,

Make no delay.

Summon all the dust to rise,

Till it stir and rubbed the eyes,

While this member jogs the other,

Each one whispering, Live you brother?

Come away,

Make this the day.

Dust, alas, no music feels

But thy trumpet, then it kneels;

As peculiar notes and strains

Cure Tarantulas raging pains.

Come away,

O make no stay!

Let the graves make their confession,

Lest at length they plead possession.

Fleshes stubbornness may have

Read that lesson to the grave.

Come away,

Thy flock doth stray.

Some to winds their body lend,

And in them may drown a friend;

Some in noisome vapors grow

To a plague and public we.

Come away,

Help our decay.

Man is out of order hurled,

Parceled out to all the world.

Lord, thy broken consort raise.

And the music shall be praise.

JUDGEMENT

Almighty Judge, how shall poor wretches brook

Thy dreadful look,

Able a heart of iron to appall,

When thou shalt call

For every man's peculiar book?

What others mean to do, I know not well;

Yet I hear tell.

That some will turn thee to some leaves therein

So void of sin

That they in merit shall excel.

But I resolve, when thou shalt call for mine,

That to decline.

And thrust a Testament into thy hand;

Let that be scanned.

There thou shalt find my faults are thine.

V.THE INNER LIFE

OUR LIFE IS HID WITH CHRIST IN GOD

My words and thoughts do both express this notion,

That Life hath with the sun a double motion;

The first is straight, and our journal friend,

The other Hide and doth obliquely bend.

One life is wrapped in flesh, and tends to earth;

The other winds towards Him whose happy birth

Taught me to live here so that still one eye

Should aim and shoot at that which Is on high,

Quitting with daily labor all My pleasure,

To gain at harvest an eternal Treasure.

THE THANKSGIVING

Oh King of grief! (A title strange, yet true,

To thee of all kings only due.)

Oh King of wounds! How shall I grieve for thee,

Who in all grief prevent me?

Shall I weep blood? Why thou hast wept such store

That all thy body was one door.

Shall I be scourged, flouted, boxed, sold?

'T is but to tell the tale is told.

My God, my God, why dost thou part from me?

Was such a grief as cannot be.

Shall I then sing, skipping thy doleful story,

And side with thy triumphant glory?

Shall thy strokes be my stroking? Thorns, my flower?

Thy rod, my posy? Crosse, my bower?

Then I will use the works of thy creation

As if I used them but for fashion.

The world and I will quarrel, and the year

Shall not perceive that I am here.

My music shall find thee, and every string

Shall have his attribute to sing,

That all together may accord in thee.

And prove one God, one harmonic.

It thou shalt give me wit, it shall appear;

If thou hast given it me, it is here.

Nay, I will read thy book and never move

Till I have found therein thy love,

Thy art of love, which I'll turn back on thee:

O my dear Savior, Victory!

Then for thy passion — I will do for that —

Alas, my God, I know not what.

THE SINNER

Lord, how I am all ague when I seek

What I have treasured in my memory!

Since if my soul make even with the week,

Each seventh note by right is due to thee.

I find there quarries of piled vanities,

But shreds of holiness, that dare not venture

To shew their face, since cross to thy decrees.

There the circumference earth is, heaven the center.

In so much dregs the quintessence is small;

The spirit and good extract of my heart

Comes to about the many hundredth part.

Yet Lord restore thine image, hear my call!

And though my hard heart scarce to thee can groan,

Remember that thou once didst write in stone.

DENIAL

When my devotions could not pierce

Thy silent ears,

Then was my heart broken, as was my verse.

My breast was full of fears

And disorder.

My bent thoughts, like a brittle bow,

Did fly asunder.

Each took his way some would to pleasures go,

Some to the wares and thunder

Of alarms.

As good go anywhere, they say.

As to be known

Both knees and heart in crying night and day,

Come come, my God, O cornel

But no hearing.

O that thou shouldn't give dust a tongue

To cry to thee,

And then not hear it crying! All day long

My heart was in my knee.

But no hearing.

Therefore my soul lay out of sight,

Untuned, unstrung.

My feeble spirit, unable to look right.

Like a nipped blossom hung

Discontented.

O cheer and tune my heartless breast,

Defer no time.

That so thy favors granting my request.

They and my mind may chime.

And mend my rhyme.

NATURE

Full of rebellion, I would die.

Or fight, or travel, or deny

That thou hast ought to do with me.

O tame my heart!

It is thy highest art

To captivate strong holds to thee.

If thou shalt let this venom lurk

And in suggestions fume and work.

My soul will turn to bubbles straight,

And thence by kind

Vanish into a wind,

Making thy workmanship deceit.

O smooth my rugged heart, and there

Engrave thy reverend law and fear!

Or make a new one, since the old

Is sapless grown,

And a much fitter stone

To hide my dust then thee to hold.

REPENTANCE

Lord, I confess my sin is great;

Great is my sin. Oh! gently treat

With thy quick flower, thy momentary bloom,

Whose life still pressing

Is one undressing,

A steady aiming at a tomb.

Man's age is two hours' work, or three.

Each day doth round about us see.

Thus are we to delights; but we are all

To sorrows old,

If life be told

From what life feel, Adam's fall.

O let thy height of mercy then

Compassionate short-breathed men!

Cut me not off for my most foul transgression.

I do confess

My foolishness;

My God, accept of my confession.

UNKINDNESS

Lord, make me coy and tender to offend.

In friendship, first I think if that agree

Which I intend

Unto my friend's intent and end.

I would not use a friend as I use Thee.

If any touch my friend, or his good name.

It is my honor and my love to free

His blasted fame

From the least spot or thought of blame.

I could not use a friend as I use Thee.

My friend may spit upon my curious floor.

Would he have gold? I lend it instantly;

But let the poor,

And thou within them, starve at door.

I cannot use a friend as I use Thee.

When that my friend pretend to a place,

I quit my interest and leave it free.

But when thy grace

Sues for my heart, I thee displace,

Nor would I use a friend as I use Thee.

GRACE

My stock lies dead, and no increase

Doth my dull husbandry improve.

O let thy graces without cease

Drop from above!

If still the sun should hide his face,

Thy house would but a dungeon prove,

Thy works night's captives. O let grace

Drop from above!

The dew doth every morning fall,

And shall the dew out-strip thy dove?

The dew, for which grass cannot call.

Drop from above.
Death is still working like a mole,
And digs my grave at each remove;
Let grace work too, and on my soul
Drop from above.
Sinne is still hammering my heart
Unto a hardness void of love;
Let supplying grace, to cross his art.
Drop from above.
O come! For thou dost know the way.
Or if to me thou wilt not move,
Remove me where I need not say.
Drop from above.

THE TEMPER

It cannot be. Where is that mighty joy
Which just now took up all my heart?
Lord, if thou must needs use thy dart,
Save that and me, or sin for both destroy.
The grosser world stands to thy word and art;
But thy diviner world of grace
Thou suddenly dost raise and race,
And every day a new Creator art.
O fix thy chair of grace, that all my powers
May also fix their reverence;
For when thou dost depart from hence,
They grow unruly and sit in thy bowers.
Scatter, or bind them all to bend to thee.
Though elements change and heaven move,
Let not thy higher Court remove,
But keep a standing Majestic in me.

A WREATH

A wreathed garland of deserved praise.
Of praise deserved, unto thee I give,
I give to thee who know all my ways.
My crooked winding ways, wherein I live.
Wherein I die, not live; for life is straight,
Straight as a line, and ever tends to thee,
To thee, who art more far above deceit
Then deceit seems above simplicity.
Give me simplicity, that I may live;
So live and like, that I may know, thy ways,
Know them and practice them. Then shall I give
For this poor wreath, give thee a crown of praise.

VI.THE CRISIS

AFFLICTION

When first thou didst entice to thee my heart,
I thought the service brave;
So many joys I write down for my part,
Besides what I might have
Out of my stock of natural delights,
Augmented with thy gracious benefits.
I looked on thy furniture so fine,
And made it fine to me;
Thy glorious household-stuff did me entwine,
And 'tice me unto thee.
Such stares I counted mine; both heaven and earth
Paid me my wages in a world of mirth.

What pleasures could I want whose King I served?

Where joys my fellows were.

Thus argued into hopes, my thoughts reserved

No place for grief or fear.

Therefore my sudden soul caught at the place.

And made her youth and fierceness seek thy face.

At first thou gave me milk and sweetness;

I had my wish and way.

My days were straw with flowers and happiness,

There was no money but May.

But with my years sorrow did twist and grow,

And made a party unawares for wo.

My flesh began unto my soul in pain,

Sicknesses cleave my bones;

Consuming agues dwell in every vein,

And tune my breath to groans.

Sorrow was all my soul; I scarce believed.

Till grief did tell me roundly, that I lived.

When I got health thou took away my life,

And more; for my friends die.

My mirth and edge was lost; a blunted knife

Was of more use then I.

Thus thin and lean, without a fence or friend,

I was blown through with every storm and wind.

Whereas my birth and spirit rather took

The way that takes the town,

Thou didst betray me to a lingering book

And wrap me in a gown.

I was entangled in the world of strife

Before I had the power to change my life.

Yet, for I threatened off the siege to raise.

Not simpering all mine age.

Thou often didst with Academic praise

Melt and dissolve my rage.

I took thy sweetened pill till I came near;

I could not go away, nor persevere.

THE ANSWER

My comforts drop and melt away like snow.

I shake my head, and all the thoughts and ends.

Which my fierce youth did bandy, fall and flow

Like leaves about me; or like summer friends,

Flies of estates and sunshine. But to all

Who think me eager, hot, and undertaking,

But in my prosecutions slack and small—

As a young exhalation, newly waking.

Scorns his first bed of dirt, and means the sky,

But cooling by the way, grows pursy and slow,

And settling to a cloud, doth live and die

In that dark state of tears — to all that so

Show me and set me, I have one reply:

Which they that know the rest, know more than.

CONTENT

Peace muttering thoughts, and do not grudge to keep

Within the walls of your own breast.

Who cannot on his own bed sweetly sleep,

Can on another's hardly rest.

Gad not abroad at every quest and call 5

Of an untrained hope or passion.

To court each place or fortune that doth fall

Is wantonness in contemplation.

Mark how the fire in flints doth quiet lie,

Content and warm it itself alone;

But when it would appear to others' eye.

Without a knock it never shone.

Give me the pliant mind, whose gentle measure

Complies and suits with all estates;

Which can let loose to a crown, and yet with pleasure

Take up within a cloister's gates.

This soul doth span the world, and hang content

From either pole unto the center;

Where in each room of the well-furnished tent

He lies warm and without adventure.

The brags of life are but a nine days' wonder.

And after death the fumes that spring

From private bodies make as big a thunder

As those which rise from a huge King.

Only thy Chronicle is lost; and yet

Better by worms be all once spent

Then to have hellish moths still gnaw and fret

Thy name in books, which may not rent:

When all thy deeds, whose brunt thou feel alone,

Were chawed by others' pens and tongue;

And as their wit is, their digestion

Thy nourished fame is weak or strong.

FRAILTY

Lord, in my silence how do I despise

What upon trust

Is styled honor riches, or fair eyes.

But is fair dust!

I surname them guild clay

Dear earth, fine grass or hay.

In all, I think my foot doth ever tread

Upon their head.

But when I view abroad both Regiments,
        The world's and thine;
Thine clad with simpleness and sad events,
        The other fine,
        Full of glory and gay weeds.
        Brave language, braver deeds;
That which was dust before doth quickly rise.
        And prick mine eyes.
O brook not this, lest if what even now
        My foot did tread.
Affront those joys wherewith thou didst endow
        And long since wed
        My poor soul, even sick of love,
        It may a Babel prove
Commodious to conquer heaven and thee
        Planted in me.

ARTILLERY

        As I one evening sat before my cell,
Me thoughts a star did shoot into my lap.
I rose and shook my clothes, as knowing well
That from small fires comes oft no small mishap.
        When suddenly I heard one say,
        Do as thou use, disobey,
Expel good motions from thy breast
Which have the face of fire, but end in rest.
I, who had heard of music in the spheres, 9
But not of speech in stars, began to muse.
But turning to my God, whose ministers
The stars and all things are, If I refuse,
Dread Lord, said I, so oft my good.
Then I refuse not even with blood

lxix

To wash away my stubborn thought;

For I will do or suffer what I ought.

But I have also stars and shooters too,

Born where thy servants both artilleries use.

My tears and prayers night and day do woe

And work up to thee, yet thou dost refuse.

Not but I am (I must say still)

Much more obliged to do thy will

Then thou to grant mine, but because

Thy promise now hath even set thee thy laws.

Then we are shooters both, and thou dost deign

To enter combat with us and contest

With thine own clay. But I would parley fain.

Shun not my arrows, and behold my breast.

Yet if thou shunned, I am thine;

I must be so, if I am mine

There is no articling with thee.

I am but finite, yet thine infinitely.

THE STAR

Bright spark, shot from a brighter place,

Where beams surround my Savior's face.

Canst thou be any where

So well as there?

Yet if thou wilt from thence depart,

Take a bad lodging in my heart;

For thou canst make a debt.

And make it better.

First with thy fire-work bum to dust

Folly, and worse then folly, lust.

Then with thy light refine,

And make it shine:

So disengaged from sin and sickness,

Touch it with thy celestial quickness,

That it may hang and move

After thy love.

Then with our trinity of light,

Motion, and heat, let's take our flight

Unto the place where thou

Before didst bow.

Get me a standing there, and place

Among the beams which crown the face

Of him who dyed to part

Sinne and my heart.

That so among the rest I may

Gutter, and curie, and wind as they;

That winding is their fashion

Of adoration.

Sure thou wilt joy, by gaining me,

To fly home like a laden bee

Unto that hive of beams

And garland-streams.

THE PRIESTHOOD

Blest Order, which in power dost so excel

That with the one hand thou lift to the sky,

And with the other throw down to hell

In thy just censures; fain would I draw nigh.

Fain put thee on, exchanging my lay-sword

For that of the holy word.

But thou art fire, sacred and hallowed fire,

And I but earth and clay. Should I presume

To wear thy habit, the severe attire

My slender compositions might consume.

I am both foul and brittle, much unfit
To deal in holy Writ.
Yet have I often seen, by cunning hand
And force of fire, what curious things are made
Of wretched earth. Where once I scorned to stand.
That earth is fitted by the fire and trade
Of skillful artists for the boards of those
Who make the bravest shows.
But since those great ones, be they near so great,
Come from the earth from whence those vessels come;
So that at once both feeder, dish, and meat
Have one beginning and one final summer
I do not greatly wonder at the sight.
If earth in earth delight.
But the holy men of God such vessels are
As serve him up who all the world commands.
When God vouch safe to become our fare.
Their hands convey him who conveys their hands.
O what pure things, most pure, must those things be
Who bring my God to me!
Wherefore I dare not, I, put forth my hand
To hold the Ark, although it seem to shake
Through the old sins and new doctrines of our land.
Only since God doth often vessels make
Of lowly matter for high uses meet,
I throw me at his feet.
There will I lie until my Maker seek
For some mean stuff whereon to show his skill.
When is my time. The distance of the meek
Doth flatter power. Lest good come short of ill
In praising might, the poor do by submission

What pride by opposition.

THE PEARL

(MATTHEW XIII, 45)

I know the ways of learning, both the head
And pipes that feed the press, and make it run;
What reason hath from nature borrowed,
Or of itself, like a good housewife, spun
In laws and policy; what the stars conspire;
What willing nature speaks, what forced by fire;
Both th' old discoveries and the new-found seas,
The stock and surplus, cause and historic;
All these stand open, or I have the keys;
Yet I love thee.

I know the ways of honor, what maintains
The quick returns of courtesy and wit;
In vies of favors whether party gains
When glory swells the heart, and mold it
To all expressions both of hand and eye,
Which on the world a true-love-knot may tie,
And bear the bundle wheresoever it goes;
How many dreams of spirit there must be
To sell my life unto my friends or foes;
Yet I love thee.

I know the ways of pleasure, the sweet strains.
The linings and the relishes of it;
The propositions of hot blood and brains;
What mirth and music mean; what love and not
Have done these twenty hundred years and more;
I know the projects of unbridled store;
My stuff is flesh, not brass; my senses live,
And grumble oft that they have more in me

Then he that curbs them, being but one to five;
Yet I love thee.
I know all these and have them in my hand;
Therefore not sealed but with open eyes
I fly to thee, and fully understand
Both the main sale and the commodities;
And at what rate and price I have thy love,
With all the circumstances that may move.
Yet through the labyrinths, not my groveling wit.
But thy silk twist let down from heaven to me
Did both conduct and teach me how by it
To climb to thee.

OBEDIENCE

My God, if writings may
Convey a Lordship any way
Whither the buyer and the seller please.
Let it not thee displease
If this poor paper do as much as they.
On it my heart doth bleed
As many lines as there doth need
To pass itself and all it hath to thee;
To which I do agree,
And here present it as my special deed.
If that hereafter Pleasure
Cavil, and claim her part and measure,
As if this passed with a reservation.
Or some such words in fashion,
I here exclude the wrangler from thy treasure.
O let thy sacred will
All thy delight in me fulfill!
Let me not think an action mine own way,

But as thy love shall sway.

Resigning up the rudder to thy skill.

Lord, what is man to thee,

That thou should mind a rotten tree?

Yet since thou canst not choose but see my actions,

So great are thy perfections,

Thou may as well my actions guide, as see.

Besides, thy death and blood

Showed a strange love to all our good.

Thy sorrows were in earnest; no faint proffer,

Or superficial offer

Of what we might not take, or be withstood.

Wherefore I all forego.

To one word only I say. No:

Where in the deed there was an intimation

Of a gift or donation

Lord, let it now by way of purchase go.

He that will pass his land,

As I have mine, may set his hand

And heart unto this deed, when he hath read.

And make the purchase spread

To both our goods, if he to it will stand.

THE ROSE

Press me not to take more pleasure

In this world of surged lies,

And to use a larger measure

Then my strict, yet welcome size.

First, there is no pleasure here;

Colored grief indeed there are.

Blushing woes, that look as clear

As if they could beauty spare.

Or if such deceits there be.
Such delights I meant to say,
There are no such things to me.
Who have passed my right away.
But I will not much oppose
Unto what you now advise,
Only take this gentle rose,
And therein my answer lies.
What is fairer then a rose?
What is sweeter? Yet it purge.
Purging enmity disclose,
Enmity forbearance urge.
If then all that world prize
Be contracted to a rose.
Sweetly there indeed it lies,
But it bite in the close.
So this flower doth judge and sentence
Worldly joys to be a scourge;
For they all produce repentance,
And repentance is a purge.
But I health, not physic choose.
Only though I you oppose,
Say that fairly I refuse.
For my answer is a rose.

AN OFFERING

Come, bring thy gift. If blessings were as slow
As men's returns, what would become of fools?
What hast thou there? A heart? But is it pure?
Search well and see, for hearts have many holes.
Yet one pure heart is nothing to bestow.
In Christ two natures met to be thy cure.

O that within us hearts had propagation,

Since many gifts do challenge many hearts!

Yet one, if good, may title to a number.

And single things grow fruitful by deserts.

In public judgments one may be a nation

And fence a plague, while others sleep and slumber.

But all I fear is lest thy heart displease.

As neither good nor one. So oft divisions

Thy lusts have made, and not thy lusts alone;

Thy passions also have their set partitions.

These parcel out thy heart. Recover these.

And thou may offer many gifts in one.

PRAISE

King of Glory, King of Peace,

I will love thee.

And that love may never cease

I will move thee.

Thou hast granted my request,

Thou hast heard me.

Thou didst note my working breast.

Thou hast spared me.

Wherefore with my utmost art

I will sing thee.

And the cream of all my heart

I will bring thee.

Though my sins against me cried.

Thou didst clear me.

And alone, when they replied,

Thou didst hear me.

Seven whole days, not one in seven,

I will praise thee.

In my heart, though not in heaven,
I can raise thee.
Thou grew soft and moist with tears.
Thou relented
And when Justice called for fears
Thou dissented
Small it is in this poor sort
To enroll thee.
Even eternity is too short
To extoll thee.

LOVE

Love bade me welcome; yet my soul drew back,
Guilty of dust and sin.
But quick-eyed Love, observing me grow slack
From my first entrance in.
Drew nearer to me, sweetly questioning
If I lacked anything.
A guest, I answered, worthy to be here.
Love said, You shall be he.
I, the unkind, ungrateful? Ah my dear,
I cannot look on thee.
Love took my hand and smiling did reply,
Who made the eyes but I?

VII. THE HAPPY PRIEST

THE CALL

Come, my Way, my Truth, my Life

Such a Way as gives us breath.

Such a Truth as ends all strife,

Such a Life as killed death.

Come, my Light, my Feast, my Strength

Such a Light as shows a feast.

Such a Feast as mends in length.

Such a Strength as makes his guest.

Come, my Joy, my Love, my Heart:

Such a Joy as none can move,

Such a Love as none can part.

Such a Heart as joys in love.

AARON

Holiness on the head,

Light and perfections on the breast,

Harmonious bells below, raising the dead

To lead them unto life and rest;

Thus are true Aarons rest.

Profaneness in my head.

Defects and darkness in my breast,

A noise of passions ringing me for dead

Unto a place where is no rest;

Poor priest thus am I dress.

Only another head

I have, another heart and breast,

Another music, making live not dead,

Without whom I could have no rest;

In him I am well dress.

Christ is my only head,
My alone only heart and breast,
My only music, striking me even dead,
That to the old man I may rest,
And be in him new dress.
So holy in my head.
Perfect and light in my dear breast,
My doctrine tuned by Christ, (who is not dead,
But lives in me while I do rest)
Come people! Aaron's dress.

THE HOLDFAST

I threatened to observe the strict decree
Of my dear God with all my power and might.
But I was told by one it could not be,
Yet I might trust in God to be my light.
Then will I trust, said I, in him alone.
Nay, even to trust in him was also his;
We must confess that nothing is our own.
Then I confess that he my succor is.
But to have ought is ours, not to confess
That we have ought. I stood amazed at this,
Much troubled, till I heard a friend express
That all things were more ours by being his.
What Adam had, and forfeited for all,
Christ keep now, who cannot fail or fall.

A TRUE HYMNE

My joy, my life, my crown!
My heart was meaning all the day
Somewhat it fain would say;
And still it run muttering up and down
With only this. My joy, my life, my crown.

Yet slight not these few words.

If truly said, they may take part

Among the best in art.

The fineness which a hymn or psalm affords

Is when the soul unto the Hues accords.

He who craves all the mind.

And all the soul, and strength, and time.

If the words only rhyme,

Justly complains that somewhat is behind

To make his verse, or write a hymn in kind.

Whereas if the heart be moved,

Although the verse be somewhat scant,

God doth supply the want.

As when the heart says (sighing to be approved)

O, could I love I and stops: God write, Loved.

THE POSY

Let wits contest,

And with their words and posies windows fill.

Less than the least

Of all thy mercies, is my posy still.

This on my ring,

This by my picture, in my book I write.

Whether I sing,

Or say, or dictate, this is my delight.

Invention rest,

Comparisons go play, wit use thy will.

Less than the least

Of all God's mercies, is my posy still.

THE QUIP

The merry world did on a day

With his train-bands and mates agree

To meet together where I lay,

And all in sport to gear at me.

First, Beauty crept into a rose;

Which when I pluck not, Sir, said she,

Tell me, I pray, whose hands are those?

But thou shalt answer, Lord, for me.

Then Money came, and chinking still.

What tune is this, poor man? said he,

I heard in Music you had skill.

But thou shalt answer. Lord, for me.

Then came brave Glory puffing by

In silks that whistled, who but he?

He scarce allowed me half an eye.

But thou shalt answer, Lord, for me.

Then came quick Wit and Conversation,

And he would needs a comfort be,

And, to be short, make an oration.

But thou shalt answer, Lord, for me.

Yet when the hour of thy design

To answer these fine things shall come.

Speak not at large, say, I am thine;

And then they have their answer home.

CLASPING OF HANDS

Lord, thou art mine, and I am thine,

If mine I am; and thine much more

Then I or ought or can be mine.

Yet to be thine doth me restore;

So that again I now am mine,

And with advantage mine the more.

Since this being mine brings with it thine,

And thou with me dost thee restore.

If I without thee would be mine,
I neither should be mine nor thine.
Lord, I am thine, and thou art mine;
So mine thou art that something more
I may presume thee mine then thine.

For thou didst suffer to restore
Not thee, but me, and to be mine,
And with advantage mine the more.
Since thou in death was none of thine,
Yet then as mine didst me restore.
O be mine still! Still make me thine!
Or rather make no Thine and Mine!

GRATEFULNESS

Thou that hast given so much to me,
Give one thing more, a grateful heart.
See how thy beggar works on thee
By art.

He makes thy gifts occasion more,
And says, If he in this be cross,
All thou hast given him heretofore
Is lost.

But thou didst reckon, when at first
Thy word our hearts and hands did crave,
What it would come to at the worst
To save:

Perpetual knockings at thy door.
Tears sullying thy transparent rooms,
Gift upon gift, much would have more,
And comes.

This notwithstanding, thou went on
And didst allow us all our noise.

Nay, thou hast made a sigh and groan
Thy joys.
Not that thou hast not still above
Much better tunes then groans can make.
But that these country-airs thy love
Did take.
Wherefore I cry and cry again,
And in no quiet canst thou be
Till I a thankful heart obtain
Of thee.
Not thankful when it please me;
As if thy blessings had spare days,
But such a heart whose pulse may be
Thy praise.

THE INVITATION

Come ye hither all whose taste
Is your waste.
Save your cost and mend your fare.
God is here prepared and dress.
And the feast,
God, in whom all dainties are.
Come ye hither all whom wine
Doth define.
Naming you not to your good.
Weep what ye have drunk amiss,
And drink this.
Which before ye drink is blood.
Come ye hither all whom pain
Doth arraign.
Bringing all your sins to sight.
Taste and fear not. God is here

In this cheer,

And on sin doth cast the fright

Come ye hither all whom joy

Doth destroy,

While ye graze without your bounds.

Here is joy that drown quite

Your delight,

As a flood the lower grounds.

Come ye hither all whose love

Is your dove.

And exalts you to the sky

Here is love which, having breath

Even in death,

After death can never die.

Lord I have invited all,

And I shall

Still invite, still call to thee.

For it seems but just and right

In my sight,

Where is all, there all should be.

THE BANQUET

Welcome sweet and sacred cheer,

Welcome dear!

With me, in me, live and dwell;

For thy neatness pass sight.

Thy delight

Pass tongue to taste or tell.

O what sweetness from the bowl

Fills my soul.

Such as is and makes divine!

Is some star (fled from the sphere)

Melted there.

As we sugar melt in wine?

Or hath sweetness in the bread

Made a head

To subdue the smell of sin;

Flowers, and gums, and powders giving

All their living,

Lest the enemy should win?

Doubtless neither star nor flower

Hath the power

Such a sweetness to impart,

Only God, who gives perfumes,

Flesh assumes,

And with it perfumes my heart.

But as Pomanders and wood

Still are good.

Yet being bruised are better scented,

God to show how far his love

Could improve,

Here, as broken, is presented.

When I had forgot my birth,

And on earth

In delights of earth was drowned,

God took blood and needs would be

Spilt with me,

And so found me on the ground.

EVEN-SONG

Blest be the God of love,

Who gave me eyes, and light, and power this day

Both to be busy and to play.

But much more blest be God above

Who gave me sight alone,
Which to himself he did deny;
For when he sees my ways, I die;
But I have got his son, and he hath none.
What have I brought thee home
For this thy love? Have I discharged the debt
Which this days favor did beget?
I ran, but all I brought was foam.
Thy diet, care, and cost
Do end in bubbles, balls of wind;
Of wind to thee whom I have cross,
But balls of wildfire to my troubled mind.
Yet still thou go on,
And now with darkness closest weary eyes,
Saying to man, It doth suffice.
Henceforth repose. Your work is done.
Thus in thy Ebony box
Thou dost enclose us, till the day
Put our amendment in our way,
And give new wheels to our disordered clocks.
I muse which shows more love,
The day or night that is the gale, this the harbor;
That is the walk, and this the arbor;
Or that the garden, this the grove.
My God, thou art all love.
Not one poor minute escapes thy breast
But brings a favor from above.
And in this love, more than in bed, I rest.

VIII.BEMERTON STUDY

PROVIDENCE

O sacred Providence, who from end to end
Strongly and sweetly moves! Shall I write,
And not of thee through whom my fingers bend
To hold my quill? Shall they not do thee right?

Of all the creatures both in sea and land
Only to Man thou hast made known thy ways,
And put the penne alone into his hand,
And made him Secretary of thy praise.

Beasts fain would sing; birds ditty to their notes;
Trees would be tuning on their native lute
To thy renown; but all their hands and throats
Are brought to Man, while they are lame and mute.

Man is the world's high Priest. He doth present
The sacrifice for all; while they below
Unto the service mutter an assent,
Such as springs use that fall and winds that blow.

He that to praise and laud thee doth refrain
Doth not refrain unto himself alone,
But robs a thousand who would praise thee fain,
And doth commit a world of sin in one.

The beasts say, Eat me; but if beasts must teach.
The tongue is yours to eat, but mine to praise.
The trees say, Pull me; but the hand you stretch
Is mine to write, as it is yours to raise.

Wherefore, most sacred Spirit, I here present

For me and all my fellows praise to thee.
And just it is that I should pay the rent,
Because the benefit accrues to me.
We all acknowledge both thy power and love
To be exact, transcendent, and divine;
Who dost so strongly and so sweetly move,
While all things have their will, yet none but thine.
Who hath the virtue to express the rare
And curious virtues both of herbs and stones?
Is there an herb for that? O that thy care
Would show a root that gives expressions!
And if an herb hath power, what have the stars?
A rose, besides his beauty, is a cure.
Doubtless our plagues and plenty, peace and wares
Are there much surer then our art is sure.
Thou hast hid metals. Man may take them thence.
But at his peril. When he digs the place.
He makes a grave; as if the thing had sense,
And threatened man that he should fill the space.
Even poisons praise thee. Should a thing be lost?
Should creatures want for want of heed their due?
Since where are poisons, antidotes are most;
The help stands close and keeps the fear in view.
The sea, which seems to stop the traveler,
Is by a ship the speedier passage made.
The winds, who think they rule the mariner,
Are niled by him and taught to serve his trade.
And as thy house is full, so I adore
Thy curious art in marshalling thy goods.
The hills with health abound; the vales with store;
The South with marble; North with furs and woods.

To show thou art not bound, as if thy lot

Were worse than ours, sometimes thou shift hands.

Most things move the under-jaw; the Crocodile not.

Most things sleep lying; the Elephant leans or stands.

But who hath praise enough? Nay who hath any?

None can express thy works but he that knows them.

And none can know thy works, which are so many

And so complete, but only he that owes them.

All things that are, though they have several ways,

Yet in their being join with one advise

To honor thee. And so I give thee praise

In all my other hymns, but in this twice.

Each thing that is, although in use and name

It go for one, hath many ways in store

To honor thee. And so each hymn thy fame

Extoll many ways, yet this one more.

DIVINITY

As men, for fear the stars should sleep and nod

And trip at night, have spheres supplied,

As if a star were duller then a clod,

Which knows his way without a guide;

Just so the other heaven they also serve,

Divinity's transcendent sky.

Which with the edge of wit they cut and carve.

Reason triumphs, and faith lies by.

Could not that wisdom which first broach the wine

Have thickened it with definitions?

And jagged his seamless coat, had that been fine,

With curious questions and divisions?

THE BRITISH CHURCH

I joy, dear Mother, when I view

Thy perfect lineaments, and hue
Both sweet and bright.
Beauty in thee takes up her place.
And dates her letters from thy face
When she doth write.
A fine aspect in fit array,
Neither too mean, nor yet too gay,
Shows who is best.
Outlandish looks may not compare,
For all they either painted are.
Or else undress.
She on the hills which wantonly
Allure all, in hope to be
By her preferred,
Hath kissed so long her painted shrines
That even her face by kissing shines,
For her reward.
She in the valley is so shy
Of dressing that her hair doth lie
About her ears;
While she avoids her neighbor's pride.
She wholly goes on the other side,
And nothing wears.
But dearest Mother, (what those miss)
The mean, thy praise and glory is
And long may be.
Blessed be God, whose love it was
To double-moat thee with his grace,
And none but thee.

CHURCH-RENTS AND SCHISMES

Brave rose, (alas!) where art thou? In the chair

Where thou didst lately so triumph and shine
A worm doth sit, whose many feet and hair
Are the more foul the more thou wert divine.
This, this hath done it, this did bite the root
And bottom of the leaves; which when the wind
Did once perceive, it blew them under foot.
Where rude unhallowed steps do crush and grind
Their beauteous glories. Only shreds of thee,
And those all bitten, in thy chair I see.
Why doth my Mother blush? Is she the rose
And shows it so? Indeed Christ's precious blood
Gave you a color once; which when your foes
Thought to let out, the bleeding did you good,
And made you look much fresher than before.
But when debates and fretting jealousies
Did worm and work within you more and more,
Your color faded, and calamities
Turned your ruddy into pale and bleak.
Your health and beauty both began to break.
Then did your several parts unloose and start.
Which when your neighbors saw, Uke a north wind
They rushed in and cast them in the dirt,
Where Pagans tread. O Mother dear and kind.
Where shall I get me eyes enough to weep,
As many eyes as stars? Since it is night.
And much of Asia and Europe fast asleep.
And even all Africa. Would at least I might
With these two poor ones luck up all the dew
Which falls by night, and pour it out for you!

THE JEWS

Poor nation, whose sweet sap and juice

Our cyans have purloined and left you dries;
Whose streams we got by the Apostles' slice
And use in baptism, while ye pine and die;
Who, by not keeping once, became a debter,
And now by keeping lose the letter;
Oh that my prayers! mine, alas!
Oh that some Angel might a trumpet sound,
At which the Church falling upon her face
Should cry so loud until the trump was drowned.
And by that cry of her dear Lord obtain
That your sweet sap might come again!

SELF-CONDEMNATION

Thou who condemn Jewish hate
For choosing Barabbas, a murderer,
Before the Lord of glory.
Look back upon thine own estate,
Call home thine eye (that busy wanderer),
That choice may be thy story.
He that doth love, and love amiss,
This world's delights before true Christian joy.
Hath made a Jewish choice.
The world an ancient murderer is;
Thousands of souls it hath, and doth destroy
With her enchanting voice.
He that hath made a sorry wedding
Between his soul and gold, and hath preferred
False gain before the true,
Hath done what he condemn in reading;
For he hath sold for money his dear Lord,
And is a Judas-Jew.
Thus we prevent the last great day.

And judge ourselves. That light which sin and passion
Did before dime and choke.
When once those snuffs are take away.
Shines bright and clear, even unto condemnation,
Without excuse or coke.

DECAY

Sweet were the days when thou didst lodge with Lot,
Struggle with Jacob, sit with Gideon,
Advise with Abraham, when thy power could not
Encounter Moses' strong complaints and mon.
Thy words were then, Let me alone.
One might have sought and found thee presently
At some fair oak, or bush, or cave, or well.
Is my God this way? No, they would reply.
He is to Sinai gone as we heard tell.
List, ye may hear great Aaron's bell.
But now thou dost thy self-immure and close
In some one corner of a feeble heart.
Where yet both Sinne and Satan, thy old foes.
Do pinch and straiten thee and use much art
To gain thy thirds and little part.
I see the world grows old, when as the heat
Of thy great love once spread, as in an urn
Doth closet up itself and still retreat.
Cold sin still forcing it, till it return,
And calling Justice, all things burn.

JUSTICE

O dreadful Justice, what a fright and terror
Was thou of old,
When sin and error
Did show and shape thy looks to me,

And through their glass discolor thee!

He that did but look up was proud and bold.

The dishes of thy balance seemed to gape,

Like two great pits.

The beam and scape

Did like some torturing engine show.

Thy hand above did burn and glow,

Panting the stoutest hearts, the proudest wits.

But now that Christ's pure vail presents the sight,

I see no fears.

Thy hand is white,

Thy scales like buckets, which attend

And interchangeably descend.

Lifting to heaven from this well of tears.

For where before thou still didst call on me.

Now I still touch

And harp on thee.

God's promises have made thee mine.

Why should I justice now decline?

Against me there is none, but for me much.

CONSTANCY

Who is the honest man?

He that doth still and strongly good pursue,

To God, his neighbor, and himself most true.

Whom neither force nor fawning can

Unpin or wrench from giving all their due.

Whose honesty is not

So loose or easy that a ruffling wind

Can blow away, or glittering look it blind.

Who rides his sure and even trot

While the world now rides by, now lags behind.

Who, when great trials come.

Nor seeks nor shuns them; but doth calmly stay

Till he the thing and the example weigh.

All being brought into a sum.

What place or person calls for, he doth pay.

Whom none can work or woe

To use in anything a trick or sleight.

For above all things he abhors deceit.

His words and works and fashion too

All of a piece, and all are clear and straight.

Who never melts or thaws

At close temptation. When the day is done,

His goodness sets not, but in dark can run.

The sun to others write laws,

And is their virtue. Virtue is his Sun.

Who, when he is to treat

With sick folks, women, those whom passions sway.

Allows for that and keeps his constant way.

Whom others' faults do not defeat;

But though men fail him, yet his part doth play.

Whom nothing can procure.

When the wide world runs bias, from his will

To writhe his limbs, and share, not mend the ill.

This is the Mark-man, safe and sure.

Who still is right, and prays to be so still.

THE FOIL

If we could see below

The sphere of virtue and each shining grace

As plainly as that above doth show,

This were the better sky, the brighter place.

God hath made stars the foil

To set off virtues, grief to set off sinning.

Yet in this wretched world we toil

As if grief were not foul, nor virtue winning.

MAN'S MEDLEY

Hear, how the birds do sing.

And woods do ring!

All creatures have their joy, and man hath his.

Yet if we rightly measure,

Man's joy and pleasure

Rather hereafter then in present is.

To this life things of sense

Make their pretense;

In the other Angels have a right by birth.

Man ties them both alone,

And makes them one.

With the one hand touching heaven, with the other earth.

In soul he mounts and flies.

In flesh he dies.

He wears a stuff whose thread is coarse and round,

But trimmed with curious lace,

And should take place

After the trimming, not the stuff and ground.

Not that he may not here

Taste of the cheer;

But as birds drink and straight lift up their head,

So must he sip and think

Of better drink

He may attain to after he is dead.

But as his joys are double,

So is his trouble.

He hath two winters, other things but one.

Both frosts and thoughts do nip

And bite his lip,

And he of all things fears two deaths alone.

Yet even the greatest grief

May be reliefs,

Could he but take them right and in their ways.

Happy is he whose heart

Hath found the art

To turn his double pains to double praise.

GIDDINESS

Oh, what a thing is man! How far from power,

From settled peace and rest!

He is some twenty several men at least

Each several hours.

One while he counts of heaven as of his treasure;

But then a thought creeps in

And calls him coward who for fear of sin

Will lose a pleasure.

Now he will fight it out and to the wares;

Now eat his bread in peace

And smudge in quiet. Now he scorns increase;

Now all day spares.

He builds a house, which quickly down must go.

As if a whirlwind blew

And crush the building; and it's partly true,

His mind is so.

O what a sight were Man if his attires

Did alter with his mind;

And like a Dolphin's skin, his clothes combined

With his desires!

Surely if each one saw another's heart.

There would be no commerce,
No sale or bargain pass. All would disperse,
And live apart.
Lord, mend or rather make us. One creation
Will not suffice our turn.
Except thou make us daily, we shall spurn
Our own salvation.

BUSINESS

Canst be idle? Canst thou play.
Foolish soul, who sinned today?
Rivers run, and springs each one
Know their home, and get them gone.
Hast thou tears, or hast thou none?
If, poor soul, thou hast no tears,
Would thou had no faults or fears!
Who hath these, those ill forbears.
Winds still work; it is their plot,
Be the season cold or hot.
Hast thou sighs, or hast thou not?
If thou hast no sighs or groans.
Would thou had no flesh and bones!
Lesser pains scape greater ones.
But if yet thou idle be,
Foolish soul, who did for thee?
Who did leave his Father's throne
To assume thy flesh and bone?
Had he life, or had he none?
If he had not lived for thee,
Thou had did most wretchedly,
And two deaths had been thy fee.
He so far thy good did plot

That his own self he forgot.

Did he die, or did he not?

If he had not did for thee.

Thou had lived in misery.

Two lives worse than ten deaths be.

And hath any space of breath

'Twixt his sins and Savior's death?

He that lose gold, though dross.

Tells to all he meets his cross.

He that sins, hath he no loss?

He that finds a silver vein

Thinks on it, and thinks again.

Brings thy Savior's death no gain?

Who in heart not ever kneels

Neither sin nor Savior feels.

THE PULLEY

When God at first made man,

Having a glass of blessings standing by,

Let us (said he) pour on him all we can.

Let the world's riches, which dispersed lie.

Contract into a span.

So strength first made a way.

Then beauty flowed, then wisdom, honor, pleasure.

When almost all was out, God made a stay,

Perceiving that alone of all his treasure

Rest in the bottom lay.

For if I should (said he)

Bestow this jewel also on my creature,

He would adore my gifts instead of me.

And rest in Nature, not the God of Nature.

So both should losers be.

Yet let him keep the rest,

But keep them with repining restlessness.

Let him be rich and weary, that at least.

If goodness lead him not, yet weariness

May toss him to my breast.

MARIE MAGDALENE

When blessed Marie wiped her Savior's feet,

(Whose precepts she had trampled on before)

And wore them for a Jewell on her head,

Shewing his steps should be the street

Wherein she thenceforth evermore

With pensive humbleness would live and tread;

She being stained herself, why did she strive

To make him clean who could not be defiled?

Why kept she not her tears)for her own faults.

And not his feet? Though we could dive

In tears like seas, our sins are piled

Deeper then they, in words, and works, and thoughts.

Dear soul, she knew who did vouchsafe and deign

To bear her filth, and that her sins did dash

Even God himself; wherefore she was not loth,

As she had brought wherewith to stain,

So to bring in wherewith to wash.

And yet, in washing one, she washed both.

THE AGONY

Philosophers have measured mountains,

Fathomed the depths of seas, of states, and kings,

Walked with a staff to heaven, and traced fountains;

But there are two vast, spacious things,

The which to measure it doth more believe,

Yet few there are that sound them Sinne and Love.

Who would know Sinne, let him repair

Unto Mount Olivet; there shall he see

A man so wrung with pains that all his hair,

His skin, his garments blood be.

Sinne is that press and vice which force pain

To hunt his cruel food through every vein.

Who knows not Love, let him assay

And taste that juice which on the cross a pike

Did set again a broach; then let him say

If ever he did taste the like.

Love is that liquor sweet and most divine

Which my God feels as blood; but I, as wine.

THE BAG

Away despair! My gracious Lord doth hear.

Though winds and waves assault my keel,

He doth preserve it; he doth steer,

Even when the boat seems most to reel.

Storms are the triumph of his art.

Well may he close his eyes, but not his heart.

Hast thou not heard that my Lord Jesus did?

Then let me tell thee a strange story.

The God of power, as he did ride

In his majestic robes of glory,

Resolved to light; and so one day

He did descend, undressing all the way.

The stares his tire of light and rings obtained,

The cloud his bow, the fire his spear,

The sky his azure mantle gained.

And when they asked what he would wear.

He smiled and said, as he did go.

He had new clothes a making here below.

When he was come, as travelers are wont,

He did repair unto an in.

Both then and after, many a brunt

He did endure to cancel sin.

And having given the rest before.

Here he gave up his life to pay our score.

But as he was returning, there came one

That ran upon him with a spear.

He who came hither all alone.

Bringing nor man, nor arms, nor fear,

Received the blow upon his side;

And straight he turned and to his brethren cried,

If ye have anything to send or write,

(I have no bag, but here is room)

Unto my father's hands and sight

(Believe me) it shall safely come.

That I shall mind what you impart,

Look, you may put it very near my heart.

Or if hereafter any of my friends

Will use me in this kind, the door

Shall still be open; what he sends

I will present, and somewhat more,

Not to his hurt. Sighs will convey

Anything to me. Hear despair, away!

LOVE-JOY

As on a window late I cast mine eye,

I saw a vine drop grapes with J and C

Annealed on every bunch. One standing by

Asked what it meant. I (who am never loth

To spend my judgment) said, It seemed to me

To be the body and the letters both

Of Joy and Charity. Sir, you have not missed,
The man replied: It figures JESUS CHRIST.

IX.RESTLESSNESS
LOVE UNKNOWN

Dear Friend, sit down, the tale is long and sad,
And in my fainting I presume your love
Will more comply then help. A Lord I had.
And have, of whom some grounds which may improve
I hold for two lives, and both lives in me.
To him I brought a dish of fruit one day.
And in the middle placed my heart. But he
(I sigh to say)
Looked on a servant who did know his eye
Better then you know me, or (which is one) 10
Then I myself. The servant instantly.
Quitting the fruit, seized on my heart alone
And threw it in a font wherein did fall

A stream of blood which issued from the side
Of a great rock. I well remember all
And have good cause. There it was dipped and did,
And washed and wrung; the very wringing yet
Enforce tears. Your heart was foul, I fear.

Indeed 'tis true. I did and do commit
Many a fault more than my lease will bear,
Yet still ask pardon and was not denied.
But you shall hear. After my heart was well,
And clean and fair, as I one even-tide
(I sigh to tell)
Walked by myself abroad, I saw a large
And spacious fornace flaming, and thereon
A boiling caldron round about whose verge
Was in great letters set AFFLICTION.

The greatness showed the owner. So I went
To fetch a sacrifice out of my fold,
Thinking with that which I did thus present
To warm his love, which I did fear grew cold.

But as my heart did tender it, the man
Who was to take it from me slipped his hand
And threw my heart into the scalding pan—
My heart, that brought it (do you understand?)
The offerers heart. Your heart was hard, I fear.

Indeed it is true. I found a callous matter
Began to spread and to expatiate there;
But with a richer drug then scalding water
I bathed it often, even with holy blood.
Which at a board, while many drunk bare wine,
A friend did steal into my cup for good,
Even taken inwardly, and most divine

To supple hardness. But at the length
Out of the caldron getting, soon I fled
Unto my house, where to repair the strength
Which I had lost, I hasted to my bed.
But when I thought to sleep out all these faults
(I sigh to speak)
I found that some had stuffed the bed with thoughts,
I would say thorns. Dear, could my heart not break,
When with my pleasures even my rest was gone?
Full well I understood who had been there,
For I had given the key to none but one.
It must be he. Your heart was dully I fear.
Indeed a slack and sleepy state of mind
Did oft possess me, so that when I prayed.
Though my lips went, my heart did stay behind.
But all my scores were by another paid,
Who took the debt upon him. Truly, Friend,
For ought I hear, your Master shows to you
More favor then you worth of. Mark the end:
The Font did only what was old renew,
The Caldron supplied what was grown too hard.
The Thorns did quicken what was grown too dull.
All did but strive to mend what you had marred.
Wherefore be cheered, and praise him to the full
Each day, each hour, each moment of the week.
Who fain would have you be new, tender, quick.

THE FAMILY

What doth this noise of thoughts within my heart.
As if they had a part?
What do these loud complaints and pulling fears,
As if there were no rule or ears?

But, Lord, the house and family are thine,
Though some of them repine.
Turn out these wranglers which defile thy seat,
For where thou dwell all is neat.
First Peace and Silence all disputes control,
Then Order plays the soul;
And giving all things their set forms and hours.
Makes of wild woods sweet walks and bowers.
Humble Obedience near the door doth stand,
Expecting a command;
Then whom in waiting nothing seems more slow,
Nothing more quick when she doth go.
Joys oft are there, and grief as oft as joys,
But grief without a noise;
Yet speak they louder than distempered fears.
What is so shrill as silent tears?
This is thy house, with these it doth abound.
And where these are not found,
Perhaps thou come sometimes and for a day,
But not to make a constant stay.

THE DISCHARGE

Busy enquiring heart, what wouldst thou know?
Why dost thou pry.
And turn, and leer, and with a chorus eye
Look high and low.
And in thy looking stretch and grow?
Hast thou not made thy counts and summed up all?
Did not thy heart
Give up the whole and with the whole depart?
Let what will fall.
That which is past who can recall?

Thy life is God's, thy time to come is gone.

And is his right.

He is thy night at noon, he is at night

Thy noon alone.

The crop is his, for he hath sown.

And well it was for thee, when this befell.

That God did make

Thy business his, and in thy life partake;

For thou canst tell.

If it be his once, all is well.

Things present shrink and die. But they that spend

Their thoughts and sense

On future grief, do not remove it thence.

But it extend,

And draw the bottom out an end.

God chains the dog till night. Wilt loose the chain.

And wake thy sorrow?

Wilt thou forestall it, and now grieve tomorrow,

And then again

Grieve over freshly all thy pain?

Either grief will not come, or if it must,

Do not forecast.

And while it cometh it is almost past.

Away distrust!

My God hath promised, he is just.

THE SIZE

Content thee, greedy heart.

Modest and moderate joys to those that have

Title to more hereafter when they part,

Are passing brave.

Let the upper springs into the low

Descend and fall, and thou dost flow

What though some have a fraught

Of cloves and nutmegs, and in cinnamon sail;

If thou hast wherewithal to spice a draught,

When grief prevail,

And for the future time art heir

To the Isle of spices, isn't not fair?

To be in both worlds full

Is more than God was, who was hungry here.

Wouldst thou his laws of fasting?

Enact good cheer?

Lay out thy joy, yet hope to save it?

Wouldst thou both eat thy cake and have it?

Great joys are all at once,

But little do reserve themselves for more.

Those have their hopes; these what they have renounce,

And live on score.

Those are at home, these journey still

And meet the rest on Sion's hill.

Thy Savior sentenced joy,

And in the flesh condemned it as unfit,

At least in lump, for such doth oft destroy;

Whereas a bit

Doth tice us on to hopes of more.

And for the present health restore.

A Christian's state and case

Is not a corpulent, but a thin and spare

Yet active strength; whose long and bony face

Content and care

Do seem to equally divide—

Like a pretender, not a bride.

Wherefore sit down, good heart.

Grasp not at much, for fear thou lose all.

If comforts fell according to desert,

They would great frosts and snows destroy;

For we should count, Since the last joy.

Then close again the seam

Which thou hast opened. Do not spread thy robe

In hope of great things. Call to mind thy dream,

An earthly globe,

On whose meridian was engrave.

These seas are tears, and heaven the haven.

THE METHOD

Poor heart, lament.

For since thy God refuse still.

There is some rub, some discontent,

Which cools his will.

Thy Father could

Quickly effect what thou dost move.

For he is Power; and sure he would.

For he is Love.

Go search this thing.

Tumble thy breast and turn thy book.

If thou had lost a glove or ring,

Wouldst thou not look?

What do I see

Written above there? Yesterday

I did behave me carelessly

When I did fray.

And should God's ear

To such indifference chained be

Who do not their own motions hear?

Is God less free?

But stay! What's there?

Late when I would have something done,

I had a motion to forbear.

Yet I went on.

And should God's ears

Which needs not man, be tied to those

Who hear not him, but quickly hear

His utter foes?

Then once more pray.

Down with thy knees, up with thy voice.

Seek pardon first, and God will say,

Glad heart rejoice.

HOPE

I gave to Hope a watch of mine; but he

An anchor gave to me.

Then an old prayer-book I did present;

And he an optic sent.

With that I gave a vial full of tears;

But he a few green ears.

Ah Loyterer! I'll no more, no more I'll bring.

I did expect a ring.

SUBMISSION

But that Thou art my wisdom, Lord,

And both mine eyes are thine,

My mind would be extremely stirred

For missing my design.

Were it not better to bestow

Some place and power on me?

Then should thy praises with me grow,

And share in my degree.

But when I thus dispute and grieve,

I do resume my sight,

And pilfring what I once did give,

Disseize thee of thy right.

How know I, if thou should me raise.

That I should then raise thee?

Perhaps great places and thy praise

Do not so well agree.

Wherefore unto my gift I stand;

I will no more advise.

Only do thou lend me a hand.

Since thou hast both mine eyes.

THE COLLAR

I struck the board, and cried, No more!

I will abroad.

What? Shall I ever sigh and pine?

My lines and life are free, free as the rode,

Loose as the wind, as large as store.

Shall I be still in suit?

Have I no harvest but a thorn

To let me blood, and not restore

What I have lost with cordial fruit?

Sure there was wine

Before my sighs did dry it. There was corn

Before my tears did drown it.

Is the year only lost to me?

Have I no bays to crown it?

No flowers, no garlands gay? All blasted?

All wasted?

Not so, my heart! But there is fruit,

And thou hast hands.

Recover all thy sigh-blown age

On double pleasures. Leave thy cold dispute

Of what is fit and not. Forsake thy cage,

Thy rope of sands.

Which petty thoughts have made, and made to thee

Good cable, to enforce and draw.

And be thy law,

While thou didst wink and wouldst not see.

Away! Take heed!

I win abroad.

Call in thy death's head there. Tie up thy fears.

He that forbears

To suit and serve his need

Deserves his load.

But as I raved and grew more fierce and wild

At every word.

My thoughts I heard one calling, Child!

And I replied, My Lord.

THE BUNCH OF GRAPES

Joy, I did lock thee up, but some bad man

Hath let thee out again;

And now, me thinks, I am where I began

Seven years ago. One vogue and vein,

One air of thoughts usurps my brain.

I did toward Canaan draw, but now I am

Brought back to the Red sea, the sea of shame.

For as the Jews of old by God's command

Travelled and saw no town,

So now each Christian hath his journeys spanned

Their story pens and sets us down.

A single deed is small renown.

God's works are wide, and let in future times.

His ancient justice overflows our crimes

Then have we too our guardian fires and clouds.

Our Scripture-dew drops fast.

We have our sands and serpents, tents and Crowd.

Alas! Our murmurings come not last.

But where's the cluster. Where's the taste

Of mine inheritance? Lord, if I must borrow,

Let me as well take up their joy as sorrow.

But can he want the grape who hath the wine?

I have their fruit and more.

Blessed be God, who prospered Noah's vine

And made it bring forth grapes good store.

But much more him I must adore

Who of the law's sour juice sweet wine did make,

Even God himself being pressed for my sake.

ASSURANCE

O spiteful bitter thought!

Bitterly spiteful thought! Couldn't thou invent

So high a torture? Is such poison bought?

Doubtless but in the way of punishment,

When wit contrives to meet with thee,

No such rank poison can there be.

Thou said but even now

That all was not so fair as I conceived

Betwixt my God and me: that I allow

And coin large hopes, but that I was deceived;

Either the league was broke or near it,

And that I had great cause to fear it.

And what to this? What more

Could poison, if it had a tongue, express?

What is thy aim? Wouldst thou unlock the door
To cold despairs and gnawing pensiveness?
Wouldst thou raise devils? I see, I know,
I writ thy purpose long ago.

THE CROSS

What is this strange and uncouth thing?
To make me sigh, and seek, and faint, and die,
Until I had some place where I might sing,
And serve thee; and not only I,
But all my wealth and family might combine
To set thy honor up as our design.
And then when after much delay.
Much wrestling, many a combat, this dear end,
So much desired, is given, to take away
My power to serve thee! To unbend
All my abilities, my designs confound.
And lay my threatening bleeding on the ground!
One ague dwell in my bones.
Another in my soul (the memory
What I would do for thee if once my grone
Could be allowed for harmonic).
I am in all a weak disabled thing.
Save in the sight thereof where strength doth sting.
Besides, things sort not to my will
Even when my will doth study thy renown.
Thou turn the edge of all things on me still,
Taking me up to throw me down.
So that even when my hopes seem to be sped
I am to grief alive, to them as dead.
To have my aim, and yet to be
Farther from it then when I bent my bow;

To make my hopes my torture and the fee

Of all my woes another woe.

Is in the midst of delicate to need.

And even in Paradise to be a weed.

Ah my dear Father, ease my smart!

These contrarieties crush me. These cross actions

Doe wind a rope about, and cut my heart.

And yet since these thy contradictions

Are properly a cross felt by thy son —

With but four words, my words, Thy will be done.

THE PILGRIMAGE

I travelled Oil, Seeing the hill where lay

My expectation.

A long it was and weary way.

The gloomy cave of Desperation

I left on the one, and on the other side

The rock of Pride.

And so I came to fancy's meadow straw

With many a flower.

Fain would I here have made abode,

But I was quickened by my hour.

So to care's cops I came, and there got through

With much ado.

That led me to the wild of passion, which

Some call the world;

A wasted place, but sometimes rich.

Here I was robbed of all my gold

Save one good Angell, which a friend had tied

Close to my side.

At length I got unto the gladsome hill,

Where lay my hope,

Where lay my heart. And climbing still.

When I had gained the brow and top,

A lake of brackish waters on the ground

Was all I found.

With that abashed and struck with many a sting

Of swarming fears,

I fell and cried, Alas my King!

Can both the way and end be tears?

Yet taking heart I rose, and then perceived

I was deceived;

My hill was further. So I flung away,

Yet heard a cry

Just as I went, None goes that way

And lives! If that be all, said I,

After so foul a journey death is fair,

And but a chair.

X.SUFFERING

BITTERSWEET

Ah my dear angry Lord,

Since thou dost love, yet strike,

Cast down, yet help afford,

Sure I will do the like.

I will complain, yet praise;

I will bewail, approve;

And all my sour-sweet days

I win lament, and love.

JUSTICE

I cannot skill of these thy ways.

Lord, thou didst make me, yet thou wound me;

Lord, thou dost wound me, yet thou dost relieve me;

Lord, thou relieve, yet I die by thee;

Lord, thou dost kill me, yet thou dost reprieve me.

But when I mark my life and praise.

Thy justice me most fitly pays;

For I do praise thee, yet I praise thee not;

My prayers mean thee, yet my prayers stray;

I would do well, yet sin the hand hath got;

My sold doth love thee, yet it loves delay,

I cannot skill of these my ways.

CONFESSION

O what a cunning guest

Is this same grief! Within my heart I made

Closets; and in them many a chest;

And like a master in my trade,

In those chests, boxes; in each box, a till;

Yet grief knows all, and enters when he will.

No screw, no piercer can

Into a piece of timber work and wind

As God's afflictions into man,

When he a torture hath designed.

They are too sub-still for the subtlest hearts.

And fall, like rhymes, upon the tender parts.

We are the earth, and they,

Like moles within us, heave, and cast about;

And till they foot and clutch their prey

They never cool, much less give out.

No smith can make such locks but they have keys.

Closets are halls to them; and hearts, high-ways.

Only an open breast

Doth shut them out, so that they cannot enter.

Or, if they enter, cannot rest

But quickly seek some new adventure.

Smooth open hearts no fastening have, but fiction

Doth give a hold and handle to affliction.

Wherefore my faults and sins,

Lord, I acknowledge. Take thy plagues away.

For since confession pardon wins,

I challenge here the brightest day,

The clearest diamond. Let them do their best.

They shall be thick and cloudy to my breast.

SION

Lord, with what glory was thou served of old,

When Solomon's temple stood and flourished!

Where most things were of purest gold.

The wood was all embellished

With flowers and carvings, mystical and rare.

All showed the builder's, craved the seer's care.

Yet all this glory, all this pomp and state

Did not affect thee much, was not thy aim;

Something there was that sowed debate.

Wherefore thou quit thy ancient claim,

And now thy Architecture meets with sin;

For all thy frame and fabric is within.

There thou art struggling with a peevish heart,

Which sometimes cross thee, thou sometimes it.

The fight is hard on either part.

Great God doth fight, he doth submit.

All Solomon's sea of brass and world of stone

Is not so dear to thee as one good grone.

And truly brass and stones are heavy things,

Tombs for the dead, not temples fit for thee.

But grone are quick and full of wings,

And all their motions upward be.

And ever as they mount, like larks they sing.

The note is sad, yet music for a king.

COMPLAINING

Do not beguile my heart.

Because thou art

My power and wisdom. Put me not to shame.

Because I am

Thy clay that weeps, thy dust that calls.

Thou art the Lord of glory.

The deed and story

Are both thy due. But I a silly fly

That live or die

According as the weather falls.

Art thou all justice, Lord?

Shows not thy word

More attributes? Am I all throat or eye.

To weep or cry?

Have I no parts but those of grief?

Let not thy wrathful power

Afflict my hour.

My inch of life. Or let thy gracious power

Contract my hour,

That I may climb and find relief.

AFFLICTION

My heart did heave, and there came forth, O God!

By that I knew that thou was in the grief,

To guide and govern it to my relief,

Making a scepter of the rod.

Had thou not had thy part,

Sure the unruly sigh had broke my heart.

But since thy breath gave me both life and shape,

Thou knows my tallies; and when there's assigned

So much breath to a sigh, what's then behind?

Or if some years with it escape,

The sigh then only is

A gale to bring me sooner to my bliss.

Thy life on earth was grief, and thou art still

Constant unto it, making it to be

A point of honor now to grieve in me,

And in thy members suffer ill.

They who lament one cross

Thou dying daily, praise thee to thy loss.

LONGING

With sick and famished eyes,

With doubling knees and weary bones,

To thee my cries.

To thee my grone.

To thee my sighs, my tears ascend

No end?

My throat, my soul is hoarse.

My heart is withered like a ground

Which thou dost curse.

My thoughts turn round

And make me giddy. Lord, I fall.

Yet call.

From thee all pity flows.

Mothers are kind because thou art.

And dost dispose

To them a part.

Their infants them, and they suck thee

More free.

Bowels of pity, hear!

Lord of my soul, love of my mind,

Bow down thine ear!

Let not the wind

Scatter my words, and in the same

Thy name!

Look on my sorrows round!

Mark well my furnace! O what flames,

What heats abound!

What grief, what shames!

Consider, Lord! Lord, bow thine ear

And heard

Lord Jesus, thou didst bow

Thy dying head upon the tree;

O be not now

More dead to me!

Lord hear! Shall he that made the ear,

Not hear?

Behold, thy dust doth stir.

It moves, it creeps, it aims at thee.

Wilt thou defer

To succor me,

Thy pile of dust, wherein each cram

Says, Come?

But now both sin is dead,

And all thy promises live and bide.

That wants his head;

These speak and chide,

And in thy bosom pour my tears

As theirs.

Lord Jesus, hear my heart.

Which hath been broken now so long,

That every part

Hath got a tongue!

Thy beggars grow; rid them away

Today.

My love, my sweetness, hear!

By these thy feet, at which my heart

Lies all the year.

Pluck out thy dart

And heal my troubled breast which cries.

Which dyes.

THE GLIMPSE

Whither away delight?

Thou can but now; wilt thou so soon depart,

And give me up to night?

For many weeks of lingering pain and smart

But one half hour of comfort for my heart?

Me thinks delight should have

More skill in music and keep better time.

Wert thou a wind or wave,

They quickly go and come with lesser crime.

Flowers look about, and die not in their prime.

Thy short abode and stay

Feeds not, but address to the desire of meat.

Lime begged of old (they say)

A neighbor spring to cool his inward heat,

Which by the spring's access grew much more great.

In hope of thee my heart

Picked here and there a crammed, and would not die;

But constant to his part

When as my fears foretold this, did reply,

A slender thread a gentle guest will tie.

Yet if the heart that wept

Must let thee go, return when it doth knock.

Although thy heap be kept

For future times, the droppings of the stock

May oft break forth, and never break the lock.

If I have more to spin,

The wheel shall go so that thy stay be short.

Thou know how grief and sin

Disturb the work. O make me not their sport,

Who by thy coming may be made a court!

A PARODY

Soul's joy, when thou art gone,

And I alone—

Which cannot be,

Because thou dost abide with me

And I depend on thee—

Yet when thou dost suppress

The cheerfulness

Of thy abode,

And in my powers not stir abroad,

But leave me to my load;

O what a damp and shade

Doth me invade!

No stormy night

Can so afflict or so affright

As thy eclipsed light.

Ah Lord! Do not withdraw,

Lest want of aw

Make Sinne appear,

And when thou dost but shine less clear,

Say that thou art not here.

And then what life I have,

While Sinne doth rave.

And falsely boast

That I may seek but thou art lost.

Thou, and alone thou, knows.

O what a deadly cold

Doth me enfold!

I half believe

That Sinne says true. But while I grieve,

Thou come and dost relieve.

JOSEPH'S COAT

Wounded I sing, tormented I indigent,

Thrown down I fall into a bed and rest.

Sorrow hath changed its note; such is his will

Who change all things as him please best.

For well he knows if but one grief and smart

Among my many had his full career,

Sure it would carry with it even my heart.

And both would run until they found a bier

To fetch the body, both being due to grief.

But he hath spoiled the race, and given to anguish

One of Joy's coats, enticing it with relief

To linger in me, and together languish.

I live to shew his power who once did bring

My joys to weep, and now my grief to sing.

THE FLOWER

How fresh, O Lord, how sweet and clean
Are thy returns! Even as the flowers in spring.
To which, besides their own demean.
The late-past frosts tributes of pleasure bring.
Grief melts away
Like snow in May,
As if there were no such cold thing.
Who would have thought my shrived heart
Could have recovered greenness? It was gone
Quite underground, as flowers depart
To see their mother-root when they have blown;
Where they together
All the hard weather,
Dead to the world, keep house unknown.
These are thy wonders, Lord of power,
Killing and quickening, bringing down to hell
And up to heaven in an hour;
Making a chiming of a passing-bell.
We say amiss.
This or that is;
Thy word is all, if we could spell.

XI.DEATH
THE FORERUNNERS

The harbingers are come. See, see their mark!
White is their color, and behold my head!
But must they have my brain? Must they dispark
Those sparkling notions which therein were bred?
Must dullness turn me to a clod?
Yet have they left me. Thou art still my God.

Good men ye be to leave me my best room,
Even all my heart, and what is lodged there.
I pass not, I, what of the rest become,
So Thou art still my God be out of fear.
He will be pleased with that ditty;
And if I please him, I write fine and witty.

Farewell sweet phrases, lovely metaphors.
But will ye leave me thus? When ye before
Of stews and brothels only knew the doors,
Then did I wash you with my tears, and more,
Brought you to Church well dress and clad.
My God must have my best, even all I had.

Lovely enchanting language, sugar-cane,
Honey of roses, whither wilt thou fly?
Hath some fond lover tied thee to thy bane ?
And wilt thou leave the Church and love a sty?
Fie, thou wilt soil thy broidered coat,
And hurt thy self and him that sings the note.

Let foolish lovers, if they will love dung,
With canvas, not with arras clothe their shame.
Let folly speak in her own native tongue.
True beauty dwells on high. Ours is a flame
But borrowed thence to light us thither.
Beauty and beauteous words should go together.

Yet if you go, I pass not. Take your way!

For, Thou art still my God, is all that ye
Perhaps with more embellishment can say.
Go birds of spring! Let winter have his fee!
Let a bleak paleness chalk the door,
So all within be livelier than before.

LIFE

I made a posy while the day ran by.
Here will I smell my remnant out, and tie
My life within this band.
But time did beckon to the flowers, and they
By noon most cunningly did steal away
And withered in my hand.
My hand was next to them, and then my heart.
I took, without more thinking, in good part
Time's gentle admonition;
Who did so sweetly death's sad taste convey,
Making my mind to smell my fatal day.
Yet surging the suspicion.
Farewell dear flowers! Sweetly your time ye spent,
Fit, while ye lived, for smell or ornament.
And after death for cures.
I follow straight without complaints or grief,
Since if my scent be good, I care not if
It be as short as yours.

GRIEF

O who will give me tears? Come all ye springs,
Dwell in my head and eyes. Come clouds, and rain.
My grief hath need of all the watery things
That nature hath produced. Let every vein
Suck up a river to supply mine eyes,
My weary weeping eyes, too dry for me

Unless they get new conduits, new supplies

To bear them out, and with my state agree.

What are two shallow foods, two little spouts

Of a less world? The greater is but small,

A narrow cupboard for my grief and doubts.

Which want provision in the midst of all.

Verses, ye are too fine a thing, too wise

For my rough sorrows. Cease, be dumb and mute,

Give up your feet and running to mine eyes,

And keep your measures for some lover's lute.

Whose grief allows him music and a rhyme.

For mine excludes both measure, tune, and time.

Alas, my God!

HOME

Come Lord, my head doth burn, my heart is sick,

While thou dost ever, ever stay.

Thy long deferring wound me to the quick.

My spirit gasp night and day.

O show thy self to me,

Or take me up to thee!

How canst thou stay, considering the pace

The blood did make which thou didst waste?

When I behold it trickling down thy face,

I never saw thing make such haste.

O show thy, &c.

When man was lost, thy pity looked about

To see what help in the earth or sky.

But there was none, at least no help without;

The help did in thy bosom lie.

O show thy, &c.

There lay thy son. And must he leave that nest.

That hive of sweetness, to remove

Thraldome from those who would not at a feast

Leave one poor apple for thy love?

O show thy, &c.

We talk of harvests; there are no such things

But when we leave our corn and hay.

There is no fruitful year but that which brings

The last and loved, though dreadful day.

O show thy, &c.

Oh loose this frame, this knot of man untie!

That my free soul may use her wing.

Which now is pinioned with mortality.

As an entangled, hampered thing.

O show thy, &c.

What have I left that I should stay and grone?

The most of me to heaven is fled.

My thoughts and joys are all packed up and gone.

And for their old acquaintance plead.

O show thy, &c.

Come dearest Lord, pass not this holy season,

My flesh and bones and joints do pray.

And even my verse, when by the rhyme and reason

The word is. Stay, says ever. Cornel

O show thy self to me.

Or take me up to thee!

THE GLANCE

When first thy sweet and gracious eye

Vouchsafe even in the midst of youth and night

To look upon me, who before did He

Weltering in sin,

I felt a sugared strange delight,

Passing all cordials made by any art,

Bedew, embalm, and overrun my heart,

And take it in.

Since that time many a bitter storm

My soul hath felt, even able to destroy,

Had the malicious and ill-meaning harm

His swing and sway.

But still thy sweet original joy.

Sprung from thine eye, did work within my soul.

And surging grief, when they grew bold, control,

And got the day.

If thy first glance so powerful be,

A mirth but opened and sealed up again,

What wonders shall we feel when we shall see

Thy full-eyed love!

When thou shalt look us out of pain,

And one aspect of thine spend in delight

More than a thousand suns disburse in light.

In heaven above.

THE DAWNING

Awake sad heart, whom sorrow ever drowns!

Take up thine eyes, which feed on earth.

Unfold thy forehead gathered into frowns.

Thy Savior comes, and with him mirth.

Awake, awake!

And with a thankful heart his comforts take.

But thou dost still lament, and pine, and cry.

And feel his death, but not his victory.

Arise sad heart! If thou dost not withstand,

Christ's resurrection thine may be,

Do not by hanging down break from the hand

Which as it rise, raise thee.

Arise, arise!

And with his burial-linen dry thine eyes.

Christ left his grave-clothes that we might, when grief

Draws tears or blood, not want an handkerchief.

TIME

Meeting with Time, slack thing, said I,

Thy sit is dull, whet it for shame.

No marvel, Sir, he did reply.

If it at length deserve some blame.

But where one man would have me grind it,

Twenty for one too sharp do find it.

Perhaps some such of old did pass,

Who above all things loved this life;

To whom thy sit a hatchet was.

Which now is but a pruning-knife.

Christ's coming hath made man thy debter.

Since by thy cutting he grows better.

And in his blessing thou art blest.

For where thou only wert before

An executioner at best,

Thou art a gardener now, and more —

An usher to convey our souls

Beyond the utmost stars and poles.

And this is that makes life so long.

While it detains us from our God.

Even pleasures here increase the wrong,

And length of days lengthen the rod.

Who wants the place where God doth dwell.

Partakes already half of hell.

Of what strange length must that needs be

Which even eternity excludes!

Thus far Time heard me patiently.

Then chafing said. This man deludes:

What do I hear before his door?

He doth not crave less time, but more.

A DIALOGUE-ANTHEME

Christian. Death

Chr. Alas, poor Death, where is thy glory?

Where is thy famous force, thy ancient sting?

De Alas poor mortally void of story,

Go spell and read how I have killed thy King,

Chr. Poor death! And who was hurt thereby?

Thy curse being laid on him, makes thee accuse.

De. Let losers talk I Yet thou shalt die;

These arms shall crush thee. Chr. Spare not, do thy worst.

I shall be one day better than before;

Thou so much worse than thou shalt be no more.

CPSIA information can be obtained
at www.ICGtesting.com
Printed in the USA
LVOW13s0013170417

531012LV00013BA/1235/P